EXTENSION EDUCATION FOR HUMAN RESOURCE DEVELOPMENT

About the Authors

Dr. Birendra Kumar is Professor of Agricultural Communication at G.B. Pant University of Agriculture and Technology, Pantnagar (U.P.). He has taught UG and PG courses in Extension Education for past two decades at Rajendra Agricultural University, Samastipur (Bihar) and G.B. Pant University of Agriculture and Technology, Pantnagar, (U.P.) and was rated as an excellent teacher. He has co-ordinated training and extension activities at the grassroot level in West Bengal and Bihar. He has been associated as resource person for national and international training for extension personnel in communication for past eleven years. He has co-authored a book *Training Methodology for Human Resource Development* and published nearly 50 research and professional review papers.

Dr. B.S. Hansra, Assistant Director General (Agri. Extn.) at the Indian Council of Agricultural Research, New Delhi had been Professor and Head, Department of Extension Education, Punjab Agricultural University, Ludhiana (Punjab). He taught UG and PG courses in extension education at P.A.U., Ludhiana for more than two decades and guided extension programmes of the University. He has authored ten books and more than 180 research and popular papers. He has been awarded National Fellow Award during 1995 by the Indian Society of Extension Education. He is closely associated with many national and international professional societies.

EXTENSION EDUCATION FOR HUMAN RESOURCE DEVELOPMENT

Birendra Kumar
Professor of Agricultural Communication
G.B. Pant University of
Agriculture and Technology,
Pantnagar (U.P.).

B.S. Hansra
Assistant Director General
(Agri. Extn.)
Indian Council of
Agricultural Research, New Delhi

CONCEPT PUBLISHING COMPANY PVT. LTD.
NEW DELHI-110059

ISBN: 978-81-7022-840-0

First Published 2000

Published and Printed by

Concept
Since 1974

Concept Publishing Company Pvt. Ltd.
A/15-16, Commercial Block, Mohan Garden,
New Delhi-110059 (India)
T : 91-11-41101460
E : publishing@conceptpub.com, *W*: www.conceptpub.com

PREFACE

EXTENSION education is no more an out-of-school education alone. The science and practice of extension has been found useful for environment, health, energy, small industries and taffic as well. There have been many changes in the way extension should be organized. Privatization of extension is seriously being considered, extension has also been added as the third dimension of general universities as well, participatory methods of extension are being tried and new informational technologies are finding application in providing useful information to farmers. The authors felt compelled to write a new text book which provides basic concepts with explanation, review of recent literature and experiences. The thrust of extension as development of human resources has been highlighted all through the logically developed six sections of the book, viz. conceptual orientation, historical prospective, communication methods and media, training, transfer of technology and philosophical basis of extension work. The book emerged out of creative experiences of teaching in classrooms. The interaction with students helped in deciding the form of presentation. We hope the students and colleagues find materials useful. We request readers to give their reactions and suggestions soon. Knowledge belongs to the world. No knowledge is exclusive. However, the authors have been greatly benefited by the knowledge generated by several past authors specially Dr. B.E. Swanson (Agricultural Extension — A reference manual), Dr. Neils Rolling (Extension Science — Information System in Agricultural Development), Dr. A. W. Vanden Ban & H.S. Hawkins (Agricultural Extension), Dr. O. P. Duhama and Dr. O. P. Bhatnagar (Education and Communication for Development), Dr. Neela Mukherjee (Participatory Rural Appraisal — Methodology and Applications) and many others.

Deep impressions of the teachings of Late (Dr.) Pobitra Kumar Sen, ex-Khaira Professor of Agriculture, Calcutta University and President, Seva Bharati, Kapgani, W.B., who provided opportunities to the first author to learn extension by working with the rural poor in a tribal setting are gratefully acknowledged.

The authors express gratefulness towards their respective organizations (G.B. Pant University of Agriculture and Technology, Pantnagar and Indian Council of Agricultural Research, New Delhi) for providing excellent milieu to write such book.

The sacrifices of the two families to keep the pens moving are deeply acknowledged. Finally, we remain deeply indebted to our departed parents who nurtured the urge for intellectual development in us.

Special mention must be made of Mr. Joshi of Joshi Stationery Mart, Pantnagar who was never tired of typing several versions of the manuscripts to our best satisfaction.

April, 1999

BIRENDRA KUMAR
B. S. HANSRA

CONTENTS

1

EXTENSION EDUCATION
Conceptual Framework

OVERVIEW

EXTENSION education, as it stands at the close of the twentieth century, has acquired an enviable status as discipline and profession responsible for initiating technological changes. It has been recognised as a discipline in its own right with distinct subject-matter areas. The contents have been dovetailed with the technologies for bringing changes in the behaviour of people with whom work is done. The range of technological areas have expanded from mere Agriculture, Home Economics or Veterinary to include Forestry, Fisheries, Agricultural Engineering, Small Industries, Energy, Traffic, Environment, etc. Extension uses communication as a tool to motivate changes in behaviour of people. As the nature of change is necessarily voluntary in nature, use of communication intervention helps in convincing people as much as enlisting their total involvement in programmes of changes. Extension is gradually incorporating many participatory methods of rural research and extension in order to become more interactive and relevant. The goal of extension education is developing human resource at the grassroots level by mobilising rural leadership, entrepreneurship and social consciousness.

Extension education has come a long way since its early rudimentary beginning in U.K. and U.S.A. The field has grown to its full bloom with varied international experiences. There is a vast repository of knowledge available today. The science and profession of extension education have been formalised and enriched by over a century's experiences. However, there is wide variation in perceptions regarding concept of extension education. Is it education or communication intervention? Can it be called as profession? These questions need to be discussed threadbare in the light of current developments.

EXTENSION

The word extension literally means stretching out something. We often refer to extension counter of a bank or extension of leave. Webster's dictionary describes extension as a branch of university for students who cannot attend university proper. The term university extension or extension of university was first commonly used in Britain. Extension was then being referred as an educational innovation to take the advantage of university to people at their door steps.

'Extension' is used in different countries with little variation but similar intention in essence. The Dutch use the word 'Voorlichting' meaning lighting the pathway. The British and German talk of advisory work (Beratung) which means expert advice though with choice to select the way. The Germans use the word 'Englightenment' (Aufklarung). They also use education (Erzichung) like in USA to teach people to solve problems themselves. The Austrians use furthering (Forderung) to mean stimulate one to go in a desirable direction which is similar to the Korean term 'Rural Guidance.' The French speak of 'Vulgarisation' which stresses the need for simplification. The Spanish use capacitation to indicate intentions to improve people's abilities, although it is used to mean training (Van Den Ban and Hawkins, 1988). In essence, there is common concern for communication of information to rural people to help them form sound opinion and good decisions. The goal is to help people to solve problems themselves. Thus, to be precise, extension is a method of non-formal education aimed at inducing behavioural changes in its clients for their increased knowledge, skills and income (Mishra, 1990).

Though emphasis of extension work in its early phases of growth, was concentrated on agriculture, soon it embraced the field of Home Science popularly known as Home economics in USA. The close relationship of farm and home inspired the home economics extension work then. Similarly, there has been a tendency to designate particular subject-matter areas with suffix extension like Home Science extension, Animal Husbandry extension, etc. This indicates diffusion of innovation of that field to its intended users (clientele). Agricultural extension, Fisheries extension or Veterinary extension refers to the branch of extension education which deals with economic and social aspects of people engaged in or associated with that field.

EXTENSION EDUCATION

Terms Extension, Agricultural extension or Extension education though look similar, carry different meanings. They should not be used interchangeably. Extension education points out the common fundamental principles, philosophy and procedures which are applied in different technological disciplines or problem areas. Extension education is the core with universal application. That is why many academic departments are now called as extension education rather than Agricultural or Veterinary education. Extension education also indicates the nature of the discipline or profession owing to its suffix 'Education'. According to Rolling (1986) 'Extension' refers to the actual work done by professional extension agents at various levels of management while 'extension education' refers to the body of knowledge concerning that work or practice.

There are numerous definitions of extension education available today. Mishra (1990) had tried to explore the accumulated wisdom of extension educators by quoting forty definitions showing a wide variety of views. There are many labels given to extension such as Education (Saville, 1965; Mosher, 1978; Supe, 1983), Communication (Rolling, 1986; Banden Van and Hawkins, 1988) Science (Leagans, 1961; Sinha, 1972; Singh, 1980). An attempt has been made below to discuss each of the aforesaid stands separately.

Extension as Education

Extension has often been linked with education in past. Most of the definitions refer to extension as an out-of-school education. Saville (1965) stated 'The aim of all extension work is to teach people living in rural areas how to raise their standard of living, by their own efforts, using their own resources of manpower and materials, with minimum of assistance from government.

Education is one of the oldest cultural traits in the history. It emerged with the appearance of first human life on this earth. The unmistakable presence of it was there although from that archaic beginning till the modern era. In the intervening period, it has been moulded by various forces of culture and society. Education, thus, is like water which has no shape but it takes the shape of container in which it is stored. Society is the container and education reflects the characteristics of the society. 'Education', in fact, is a broader term than 'schooling'. It is not limited to what they say as learning the art of earning. The ultimate aim of education in ancient India was not knowledge just to prepare for life in this world or for life beyond, but for complete realisation of self for liberation of the soul from fetters of life both present and future. The aim of education today is to prepare them for life and all-round development of human personality. It should strive for making an individual being well adjusted in his society. As man is moulded by society and in turn moulds society. Education, in fact, has been seen as the process of bringing desirable changes in the behavioural complex of human being. It can also be defined as the process of imparting or acquiring knowledge and habits through instruction or study. The individual has to learn new knowledge, new ways of thinking, feeling and doing things as he tries to adjust with his environment to make him useful.

Extension education appeared on the scene in its full bloom in the twentieth century to address to the needs of rural people for improved production and income through use of technologies. Thus, it was not just an attempt to pass on information and advice. In fact, extension work was inspired and initiated in order to take knowledge of agriculture to its users. The ruralites steeped deeply in superstitions and old traditions needed teaching of very practical kind to take up new practices. Thus, the new education with emphasis on 'learning by doing' and 'helping people to help themselves' emerged. It was not merely to pass information. Working with the community to analyse situations, identify problems and help them see affordable solutions within available resources was the motto. Such a practical education called for mobilisation of leadership within community to induce spirit of self reliance. Rural people have their own values and beliefs. The grip of conventionalism has formed deep grooves in the minds. Besides, the vocation is interlinked with social roles and norms. Hence working with people for their overall development requires a comprehensive educational programme. Extension education is voluntary in nature. It begins with existing level of people and aims to lead them to socio-economic development through co-operation and active participation. The concept of extension has combined the concern for the overall development of man with methodology and efficiency of a systematically organised educational programme. It is also known as a form of adult education. Extension education is largely non-formal in nature.

It is problem-oriented education for action and not for the sake of learning alone. It inspires involvement of farmers in the educational programmes. Farmers have different backgrounds as far as education, economic status or interests are concerned. Extension education must consider differential requirements of target population. Extension has been accepted as type of adult education enterprise with emphasis on technological changes. Thus, it become essential to arouse interests of farmers, provide them new technological knowledge and skill.

Extension has now become part and parcel of national governments. It is run by similar organizational hierarchy, work culture and procedures as in any bureaucratic organisation. Most extension programmes are decided by the top executives and implemented by grass-root workers. Village level functionaries are bogged down with the pre-fixed targets. There is almost no scope to consider needs and conveniences of farmers. Above all, extension work has now become more and more technology centred. It seems as if new technologies are the solutions of all the ills in rural areas and role of extension is one disseminating technology. Freiri (1974) has criticised this notion of disseminating technology alone vehemently. Knowledge is not extended from those who consider that they know to those who consider that they do not know. Knowledge is built-up in the relations between human being and the world, relations of transformation and perfects itself in the critical problematization of these relations. According to Freiri the most important task for extension worker is to prepare himself to raise the consciousness of people to help them see their problems and participate in finding solution.

Extension by nature is an educational practice but it has been used to disseminate information. Our extension workers are trained to teach and tell rather than to elicit views and ideas or encourage sharing of experiences among the community members (Tuazon, 1991). There is need to think about ways and means to make extension education more interactive and human focussed.

Extension as Communication Intervention

There is recent new awakening to highlight communication dimension of extension education. Extension as an educational endeavour uses communication as means. Education is meant to bring desirable change in behaviour of people. Communication is a tool to bring voluntary change in people. The success of communication as tool depends on extent of sharing of meaning between sender and receiver of messages. How can this sharing happen voluntarily without any force or manipulation. According to Van den Ban and Hawkins (1988), extension is a professional communication intervention deployed by an institution to induce change in social process. Extension makes use of communication like many other professions viz. social work, public relations, marketing, advertising.

Extension work is indeed planned and purposeful activity in order to bring desirable changes in rural people. Extension professionals use communication to convince people and advocate new changes. Extension presents new choices with reasons. However, the decision to accept or reject rests with people. Willing acceptance of people is supposed to be long lasting and indicative of positive change. However, there are many other ways to persuade people to change such as use of force, coercion, change in regulations, provision of subsidy or supplies. Rolling (1986) has pleaded that extension depends on communication for its leverage. It is becoming more acceptable for fields other than agriculture as well because most democratic nations prefer voluntary change as a policy strategy.

Communication refers to sharing of information and meaning. Communication between extension functionaries and farmers has been severely criticised for several biases. Experts claim that extension workers in developing nations have to deal with largely illiterate masses having limited exposure to other sources of information. It is no wonder if such people are persuaded to accept the viewpoints of extension workers who are technically superior. It is indeed wrong to assume that rural people are ignorant. In fact, they have their own values, wisdom and logics to pursue a particular practice. It is thus equally essential to understand indigenous knowledge, traditional wisdom and people's logic to be able to communicate effectively. Communication with rural clientele requires informal and personal approach. Every society has peculiar means of communication like sitting near tea-shop or exchanging news and views in village market, special carriers of message in social system (like barbers in Indian villages). Besides, rural people are not always open to outsiders though they may apparently agree. Thus, it requires thorough analysis of socio-cultural process to be able to communicate appropriately and effectively. However, the way extension workers communicate with rural clientele have been labelled as one way top-down approach. There is simplistic assumption that all the technologies are disseminated through extension agents, people would adopt. People are assumed to be passive recipients as if they are ignorant. The technologies available with research stations are taken as desirable and superior. Chambers (1990) categorically stated that in recent years this transfer of technology (TOT) paradigm has been increasingly questioned, even in the citadels of normal professionalism. Reductionist approach, high input packages and top-down extension had their successes in the uniform and controlled conditions of industrial and green revolution agriculture. But the sustainability of that increase is open to question and TOT does not work well with the more complex, diverse and risk-prone rain-fed agriculture of much of the poorer south.

Unfortunately, many extension workers do not get enough orientation in communication. Besides, their urban and technical background may prove as barrier. Extension workers in general have paid more attention to progressive farmers with resources to use the technologies adopted by them. The technical messages for the progressive and not so progressive or resource poor farmers did not vary in reality. It is thus clear that traditional approach to extension has been insensitive to the socio-economic differences among clientele groups. Farmer is not an empty pot in which technologies are to be poured. He is knowledgeable and experienced adult with his unique situations. He already has informal network of communication within social system. Therefore, there is definite need to understand farmer's environment, his knowledge, experiences, skills etc. before hand. If extension education aims to improve the quality of learning, increased involvement of clientele and dialogic communication is must to encourage articulation of problems. The extension workers should now assume the role of facilitator and development catalyst rather than mere disseminator of information. The extension worker needs to live in the community and understand and analyse socio-cultural environment alongwith people. Thus, he can be better equipped to communicate with the community. There are happy new trends to introduce such dialogic communication between extension workers, farmers and scientists in Farmer-First Extension approach (Modi, 1990).

Discipline of Extension Education

There are many definitions reflecting the nature of the discipline and profession of extension education as given below.

Extension education is an applied science, consisting of contents derived from researches, accumulated field experiences and relevant principles drawn from the behavioural sciences synthesized with useful technology in a body of philosophy, principles, content and methods focussed on the problems of out of school education for adults and youths (Leagans, 1961).

Extension education is an applied science. Its main base is technology which has to be introduced in the system through favourable acceptance and adoption by the people. This also necessitates a further understanding of the social system in which the technology is to be introduced (Sinha, 1974).

Extension education is behavioural science following a continuous, persuasive and discriminative educational process. It aims at affecting the behavioural components of people in a desirable direction through conviction communication and diffusion by its proven methods, principles and philosophies resulting in learning involvement of both client and change-agent systems (Dahama and Bhatnagar, 1980).

Extension education is applied behavioural science, the knowledge of which is to be applied to bring about desirable changes in the behavioural complex of human beings usually through various strategies and programmes of change and by applying the latest scientific and technological innovations (Singh, 1980).

Discipline refers to a branch of instruction/education, may it be a branch of art, science as vocation. Extension education has established itself as a discipline by virtue of systematic body of knowledge and well distinguished content of practical relevance, as detailed below

(i) *Systematic Body of Knowledge*

Extension education has its own principles, philosophy, methods and contents. The contents of extension education have been borrowed from various social/behavioural sciences like Sociology, Psychology, Rural Sociology, Social Psychology, Communication, Journalism, Management, Administration, etc. Such contents have been focussed on the problems of rural areas. The contents of extension education have certain distinguishing features as given below:

— Extension education did not begin as subject first. The extension works were initiated first and the rich experiences, wisdom and experiments led to evolution of discipline much later.

— It belongs to social science but has bias towards technology be it Agriculture, Home Science, Forestry, Fisheries, Family Welfare, Public Health Energy.

— It is largely rurally oriented though much of extension work in developed nations now focussed on urban audience too. It is problem-solving in nature, requiring professionals to diagnose problems and provide strategic solutions.

— It is inter-disciplinary in nature calling for use of other sister disciplines to solve problems of complex nature.

Science is a body of verified knowledge. It is method of study, approach or attitude that leads to systematic knowledge about how things operate. In fact, any branch of knowledge can be termed as science if it has been studied or arrived at through application of scientific methods. Extension education, though popularly known for its field activities, has a well established tradition of empirical investigation. Extension education researches make use of proven scientific methods rather than subjective individual experiences. Use of well thought out design of research and quantitative techniques of analysis have earned respectability for extension studies. Extension researches are apparently similar as those in sociology, anthropology, psychology, education, etc. and yet in many ways different due to distinctive features of the discipline or body of knowledge.

Extension education has established itself as well developed discipline. In India, it has acquired a status of its own within the fold of higher agricultural education.

(ii) *Growth of Academic Discipline in India*

The first ever post-graduate programme in extension education was started at Bihar Agricultural College, Sabour (Bihar) in 1955. The master's programme at Sabour, attracted good teachers with interest in Social Science Research. Next to start post-graduate programme was College of Agriculture, Nagpur by 1958. The most notable and well organised programme at Indian Agricultural Research Institute (IARI) came next. Though provisions had been made to specialise in agricultural extension within Master's programme (Associateship of ICAR) of Agronomy division, creation of separate department of Agricultural Extension with assistance from Ford Foundation under expert advice of legendary J. Paul Leagans of Cornell (USA) was a landmark event in the history of agricultural extension. Well-founded Ph.D. programme initiated in 1961 at IARI attracted many interested students, most of whom inservice students. Thus, the IARI is programme, with standard curriculum and thrust on research programme inspired replication of curriculum and research area in many institutions in the country. IARI also served as headquarters of Indian Society of Extension Education. Thus, the faculty members at IARI provided academic leadership all over the country. Another distinguished post-graduate programme (1961) including Ph.D. (1963) came up at Punjab Agricultural University, Ludhiana, PAU had many pluses such as well trained faculty (most of them had training/ education abroad) and focus on field programmes concerning youth work, farmers, training, etc. The courses were well designed and distincted. In past four decades since first ever post-graduate programme was launched at Sabour, the curriculum has been standardised in most SAUs. Almost all the SAUs are having post-graduate programme with emphasis on course.

A broad survey of curricula of post-graduate courses in extension education reveals many communalities. It is a norm to provide majority of courses from extension education (as listed below) followed by minor in technical subject-matter and compulsory course in statistical method. It is almost essential for most post-graduate programmes to write thesis based on original research.

Extension education courses offered at Master's level in most agricultural universities in India are as given below.

Fundamentals of Extension Education
Extension/Social Science Research
Extension Teaching Methods
Rural Sociology
Diffusion and Adoption of Innovation Administration
Extension Programme Planning and Evaluation
Extension Administration
Audio-visual Aids

At Ph.D. level, most departments offer the following courses with some variation.

Advanced Social Research Methods
Agricultural Communication
Extension Training
Dynamics of Social Change
Theory Construction/Scaling Techniques

Dynamics of Rural Leadership
Development Administration

A comparison with graduate level courses offered in USA as noted below, would indicate many commonalities. Graduate level extension education courses offered by several U.S. universities (Radha Krishna, *et al.*, 1993) are as follows :

Communication Media and Methods
Methodology of Extension Education
Leadership for Social Change
4-H and Youth Development
Community Development
Programme Planning and Evaluation
Extension Administration and Supervision
Co-operative Extension Organisation
Scientific Methods in the Study of Agricultural Extension

Eventhough the courses at Master's and Doctoral level look quite useful, there is general lament about lack of practical skills. Extension personnel, in general, have to serve as manager of developmental/ educational programmes. Thus, adequate skills in communication, training, planning, teaching and management are must. They should be well-versed in technical subject matter as well, to be able to solve field problems. That is why basic under-graduate degree in a technical area such as Agriculture, Veterinary, Fisheries, Forestry, Dairy Technology or Agricultural Engineering is a must for entry into Master's programme in extension education in an Indian University.

(iii) *Researches in Extension Education*

Research is an important requirement for continuous growth. It is important for a professional practice to be guided by science and scholarship rather than trial and error. With changing technologies and social situations, new techniques of .working with people are needed. Extension researches are needed to assess effectiveness of methods and find answer to problems faced by practitioners in the field. The quest for scientific enquiry is evident among academicians as empirical researches are being carried out right since the inception of the discipline in India.

A majority of researches in extension education are conducted by students for earning M.Sc. or Ph.D. degrees. Studies have revealed that of post-graduate theses in extension education emphasise on programme planning diffusion and adoption and communication methods and media (Singh, 1974; Jhamtani and Singh, 1980). An investigation into research papers published in *Indian Journal of Extension Education* from 1965-1987 also reveals a trend of emphasis on themes related with training, communication and diffusion. Various qualitative and quantitative techniques of data collection had been used to give scientific base. It is quite common now to use scales, test and analytical techniques. Extension researches are being encouraged in State Agricultural Universities, Indian Council of Agricultural Research and even State Departments of Agriculture. Most post-graduate departments have faculty research projects. ICAR institute have position of scientists (Agricultural Extension) who conduct problem-oriented researches in the field.

(iv) *Practical Utility*

Needless to say, the discipline of extension education has immediate practical relevance in enhancing production of food and development of human resource in the rural areas. It has proved beyond doubt that people with training and education in the discipline have been able to develop villages, encourage adoption of new technology, organise village communities and mobilise leadership.

Extension Education as Profession

A profession refers to a particular field of vocation or occupational organisation. Webster defined profession as a calling in which one professes to have acquired some special knowledge used by way of either instructing, guiding or advising others or of serving them in some act. According to Swanson (1975) "A profession is a remunerative occupation of high status. It is based on body of specialized knowledge. In it are self-directing practitioners with long, formal, training, performing socially accepted service under a code of ethics which places interest of clients above most of practitioners." There are a number of criteria that must be fulfilled to call a calling a profession (Brown, 1965 and Clark, 1965).

— It should have a body of knowledge based on scientific investigation, which its members must master in order to enter profession.
— It must have continued research and exchange of information among

members.

— It has established requirements of training and competency as a basis for entry into profession.
— It requires personal responsibility on the part of members for self-direction and self-evaluation.
— It must exhibit high standard of ethical conduct.
— The profession must show monopoly over the body of knowledge which it calls its own. Because of the complex and difficult nature of knowledge required, only members of a profession are in a position to pass intelligent judgement.
— The body of knowledge which the profession possessed is necessary for the good of the society.
— Its members organise association through which they act collectively to maintain and improve the service.
— The occupational group and its members have an esteemed position in the society to have earned the right to voice in public in areas concerned with professional concerns and competence.

Is it a Profession?

Extension education has established itself as a well developed discipline. Master's and doctoral degrees are awarded to those aspiring to specialize in it. Job-opportunities are now open to those trained post-graduates in training, rural development, sales, teaching, research and administrative jobs. There are positions of Scientists or Subject-Matter Specialists in Extension Education as well in most teaching, research and extension organisations. Besides, voluntary organisations and input organisations also advertise for positions to be filled by post-graduates in extension education. Thus, the discipline has potentialities to provide employment on the basis of knowledge and competencies. There are good reasons to believe that extension education fulfils the criteria for being called as profession, as discussed below.

(i) *Professional Society*

There is well developed Indian Society of Extension Education with members from all over the country and abroad. The society has branched into many chapters as well. It has a research-based journal, *Indian Journal of Extension Education*. The society organises regular seminars, symposia, workshops, etc. for discussion on topical themes like training, extension role of agricultural universities, extension management, etc. Besides, the society has advocated for standard curriculum, obligations for research and standards of performance of its members at various platforms. There are other professional journals also devoted to experience review and research-based articles like *Journal of Extension System* and *Agricultural Extension Review*. They serve the information needs of professionals and help in exchange of experiences.

(ii) *Continuing Research*

A profession is not dynamic if it does not have continuous research. The founding fathers of extension education have paved ways for research ever since co-operative extension service era in USA. In India it began with post-graduate research. Most post-graduate departments have faculty lead projects. Agricultural Research Institutions of the ICAR also recruit scientists of extension education to conduct extension research. Thus, extension researches have gained acceptance. Major Research funding, organisations like Council of Scientific and Industrial Research (CSIR), University Grants Commission (UGC), Indian Council of Agricultural Research (ICAR) and Indian Council of Social Science Research (ICSSR) finance researches in extension education.

(iii) *Significant Service*

One of the requirements of profession is its significant contribution to the society. In India, Extension Education has contributed in bringing about technological awareness among farmers. Over the years, farming on scientific line has been adopted. It has helped in enhancing food production. It has enabled agricultural universities and research institutions to extend its frontiers beyond their four walls. It has given orientation to agricultural research. It is in recognition of the value of extension work that the World Bank has helped in a big way in professionalising agricultural extension in country. Extension education, by virtue of its well developed content, professional society, traditions of research and significant contribution justifies itself to be a profession of repute. Extension education has the distinction of being labelled as largest problem solving educational systems. Extension experts have identified themselves more with adult education professional with a technological bias. All extension professionals make use of their technological speciality through adult education means.

Landmarks in Extension Education in India

The significant developments in Extension education in India, as illustrated below demonstrates importance of the profession.

— Eventhough activities resembling extension works had been started in India by voluntary leaders, bureaucrats and missionaries, the principles and methods of extension education were first tried on Indian soil with official collaboration under Etawah Pilot Project in Mahewa (Etawah), U.P., in 1948.

— Nation-wide programmes of extension were started with launching of community Development programme (1952), which signified the beginning of extension practice in organised manner.

— The teaching of extension education at under-graduate level started in 1950 at the college of agriculture, Calcutta University. The first post-graduate teaching programme was launched in 1955 at Bihar Agricultural College, Sabour. Probably the first Ph.D. programme on course basis was started at the Indian Agricultural Research Institute, New Delhi.

— The Indian Society of Extension Education began on 22nd June 1964 and with this *Indian Journal of Extension Education* started its publication.

— With establishment of a chain of agricultural universities, extension became one of three major activities besides teaching and research. Separate Directorate of Extension was created in each agricultural Universities. Gradually research institutes of the Indian Council of Agricultural Research created division or unit of extension and recruited scientists trained in extension education.

— The Indian Council of Agricultural Research created Division of Agricultural Extension at its headquarters under the leadership of Dy. Director General (Agricultural Extension). It runs several transfer of technology programmes like National Demonstration, Krishi Vigyan Kendra, Operational Research Projects, Lab to Land Project and Technology Refinement and Assessment through Institution-Village linkage programme. Thus, a number extension programmes were now directly implemented by the State Agricultural Universities and Research Institutes of the Indian Council of Agricultural Research.

— The first All India Coordinated Research Project in Extension Education entitled "A study on farming systems" resource utilization pattern, technological gaps and extension strategy with special reference to small and marginal farmers under different land and water situations" was sanctioned in 1977.

— The World Bank sponsored Training and Visit System or Reorganised Agricultural Extension was started in 1974 in Madhya Pradesh and Rajasthan and later extended to the most parts of the country. Thus, a radical restructuring in extension organisations has been done in recent years by way of better training, infrastructure enhanced research extension linkage and availability of communication facilities under State departments of agriculture. As a result, extension work has been systematised. Broadbasing of Agriculture extension has also been initiated by including more technical areas viz. Animal Husbandry, Fisheries, Agricultural Engineering, Horticulture and Forestry.

— Many agricultural universities have worked with Farming Systems Research/Extension or the other forms of participatory Technology Development, in collaboration with the international organisation (International Rice Research Institute, Ford Foundation, etc). Thus, there is increasing awareness of extension in technology development with farmers and scientist's participation. Of late, ICAR has launched a project for Adaptation and refinement of agricultural technologies with farmers' involvement. Thus, the idea of Farmer-First extension giving initiative to farmers, is gaining ground in India.

— ICAR has sanctioned Centre of Advanced Studies in Agricultural Extension at the Division of Agricultural Extension at IARI, New Delhi. This centre has initiated a series of training courses for extension professionals/academicians in frontier areas viz. curriculum development, advances in extension research, training technology, entrepreneurship development and work motivation, empowerment and development.

— Realising the importance of management in extension work, fullfledged Centre for Management of Agricultural Extension (MANAGE) has been created at Hyderabad. The centre has initiated efforts to develop management skills among extension personnel.

Extension as a Tool for Human Resource Development

Extension education is now recognised as important non-formal adult education enterprise with technological base. The central emphasis of extension work is on developing manpower in the rural areas so that they can absorb scientific knowledge and skills in solving their day-to-day problems. There has been variety of approaches to extension work emphasizing on different components, viz. technology, commodity, community, advisory role or service/supply or a combination of these. However, development of human resource is central to extension work. Human beings are most precious resource for any country. Each person is born with unique potentials, capabilities and limitations that never existed before.

What is HRD?

HRD is a new concept. The term was first applied in 1968 in George Washington University. It was used in Miami at the Conference of American Society of Training and Development in 1969. The term gained more importance in 1970 though as alternative term for training and development.

Rao (1992) explained that HRD is a process in which employees of an organisation are continuously helped in planned manner to acquire and sharpen capabilities that are rquired to perform various functions. With their present or expected future roles, they develop their general capabilities as individuals and discover and exploit their potential for their own and organisational development purposes, develop an organisational culture in which supervisor-sub-ordinate relationships, team work and collaboration among sub-units are strong and contribute to professional well-being, motivation and pride of employees.

Nadler (1994) defined HRD as planned and continuous effort by management to improve employee capacity levels and organisational performance through training, education and development programmes. Training includes those activities that are conducted to improve overall competence of an individual in a specific direction and beyond current job. Development involves learning opportunities aimed at individual growth but not restricted to a specific present or future job.

Thus, it can be said that above definitions of HRD are rooted in the context of organisations and employees. It is assumed that each human being is unique with potentials for development. However, one needs analysis of potentials and limitations, clear-cut goals of self-development as well as opportunities for learning and growth. HRD is an approach to facilitate both developments of competencies and creation of environment conducive to stimulate and nurture continuous growth of individuals and organisations.

What would be the focus of HRD approach at grassroots level. Rural development is complex process of catalysing social, economic and cultural factors. However, sustainable development is possible only when there is active participation of people in all aspects of the process. It is to establish conditions in which every individual has opportunities for development of potential. The cultivation of inner motivation and social consciousness is key to individual fulfilment through community action. Thus, Human Resource Development lays stress on development of individual, the family and the village community. HRD in rural areas must be understood in the socio-cultural context of the rural communities. It should focus on the development of inner resources of the individual and community. It aims to people to acquire social perspective relevant to development of community. This calls for organization of groups and creation of structure which would enable involvement of one and all in planning and implementation of programmes of development. Such group organisation calls for motivated leadership.

Mehta (1983) reported that rural poor can participate in their own development only when they are able to develop necessary skills, readiness and motivation for moving towards organising themselves in various ways and for various purposes. He listed following skills and knowledge as necessary prerequisite for encouraging participation of rural people in development.

— Skill in group work

— Readiness for identifying one's own problem with those of the community and understanding community problems as his own.

— Focus on community thinking and communityness.

— Skills in understanding and identifying important problems with a view to move towards problem solving and action planning.

— Skill in farming and managing self-help organisation.

— Awareness of legal rights and responsibilities.

— Interface with official.

Rolling (1988) has elaborated HRD approach to extension work in terms of five function viz. mobilization organisation, technical support and systems management, as detailed below :

Mobilization
Extension workers should act as animator rather than information disseminator. In true spirit of generating critical analysis of problems, they should encourage dialogue and discussion. Thus, people can visualise together the depth issues and reasons behind them. Such realisation alone can inspire them to take some concrete step for amelioration of their problems.

Organisation
People need forum to plan together and put plans in action. Existing forum may be revitalised or alternative organisations may be created to provide equal opportunity of participation.

Training
Self-development is not easy to come by. First, people need skills to work together as group. Activities need to be initiated so that people learn through mutual discussion and work. They must be made aware of their rights and responsibility.

Technological Support
Local resources and technologies should be supported with external ones with help and support from development organisation.

Systems Management
In order to install the four functions, maintain balance and ensure self-sustenance, it requires co-ordination and management.

Experiences with extension work around the world indicate that classical extension as practised by government organisation have not paid attention to human factors of development. The emphasis so far has been on dissemination of new technologies to enhance agricultural production. They also viewed traditional agricultural system as static or slow to change. However, many international organisations and scholars have been advocating for keeping farmer at the centre of all activities. Thus, extension to catalyse human resource needs a fresh approach which keeps farmer at the centre of all activities. This client-focussed and demand driven approach must begin from the community. There is urgent present need to take into account indigenous technological knowledge, network of communication at the grassroots and approaches of interaction and learning prevalent in the community. Extension in the new role would encourage farmer's initiatives in experimentation and dissemination of knowledge. Extension education can be made more natural, lively and self-sustaining by linking knowledge with socio-cultural process in the community. HRD approach to extension requires following considerations:

— Active farmer participation should be the basis of extension work.
— It should be based on philosophical orientation towards raising consciousness of people through dialogue-based participatory education.
— It should aim basically to empower people to gain competencies in dealing with their problems confidently.
— Methods used to work with farmers need to be interactive and mutually rewarding. Farmers are not objects of change. They should take part in the process through range of methods such as participatory rural appraisal, story-writing, songs, rapid rural appraisal, farmer to farmer training, village level workshops etc.
— It requires multi-institutional collaboration to be successful. Extension, research, farmers and other organisations must work hand in hand.

REFERENCES

Ban, A.W. Vanden (1982). The Challenges of Agricultural Extension in 1980's. *Indian Journal of Extension Education,* 17(3&4). pp. 1-9.

Ban, A.W. Vanden and Hawkins, H.S. (1988). *Agricultural Extension.* Longman Scientific & Technical.

Brown, M. (1965). Professional Values. *Journal of Cooperative Extension Service,* 3 (2). pp. 67-74.

Chambers, R. (1990). The small farmers is a professional, *Ceres,* 13(2), 1980, pp. 19-23.

Clark, R.C. (1965). Extension Education as Profession, *Indian Journal of Extension Education,* 1(1). pp. 9-13.

Freiri, P. (1974). Knowledge is critical appraisal of the world, *Ceres,* 4(3), pp. 46-51.

Jhamtani, A and Singh, Y.P. (1980). Directory of Degree Research in Extension (1972-78). *Division of Agricultural Extension,* IARI, New Delhi-110012.

Leagans, J. Paul (1961). Extension Education and Modernization in Leagons and Loomis (Eds) 1971: *Behavioural Changes in Agriculture : Concept and Strategies for influencing Transition.*

Mehta, P. (1983). New extension and training strategies, *Indian Journal of Extension Education,* 19(1&2), pp. 1-14.

Mishra, D.C. (1990). *New Direction in Extension Training*, Directorate of Extension, Department of Agriculture and Cooperation, Ministry of Agriculture, New Delhi.

Modi, B. (1990). Energizing the communication component in extension – A case for new pilot project. Paper presented at the World Bank Symposium, 1990.

Mosher, A. (1978). *An Introduction to Agricultural Extension*, New York, Agricultural Development Council (ADC), Singapore University Press.

Nadler, L. (1994). Human Resource Development in Leonard Nadler (Ed). *The Handbook of Human Resource Development.* John Wiley and Sons, New York, pp. 1.16 to 1.22.

Radhakrishna, R. B. ; A. W . Etling and B. E. Brown (1993). Training of Farmers and Extension Personnel in R.K. Samanta (Ed.) *Extension Strategy for Agricultural Development in 2lst Century*, Mittal Publications, New Delhi.

Rao, V.P. (1992). Human Resource Development and Training, *MDI Management Journal,* 15(1), pp. 108-111.

Rolling, N. (1986). *Extension Science – Information System in Agricultural Development*, Edinburgh Cambridge University Press.

Rolling, N. (1988). *Extension Science : Information Systems in Agricultural Development*, Cambridge University Press.

Saville, A.N. (1965). *Extension in Rural Communities, A Manual for Agriculture and Home Extension Workers*, London, Oxford University Press, Reprinted 1986, Oxford Tropical Handbook.

Singh, K.N. (1982). Challenges of Extension in Eighties, *Indian Journal of Extension Education,* 17 (1&2), pp. 1-9.

Singh, K.N. (1980). Agricultural Extension Education in ICAR, In *Handbook of Agriculture.* Chapter 16, p. 703.

Sinha, P.R.R. (1972). *Studies in Extension Education Hyderabad*, National Institute of Community Development (NICD), Hyderabad.

Sinha, P.R.R. (1973). Role of Extension Education in Farmers' Organization in Agricultural Development — A critical analysis. *Community Development and Panchayati Raj,* 5(4), 74.

Swanson, Burton E (Ed.) 1984. *Agricultural Extension, A Reference Manual*, Rome, Food & Agricultural Organisation (FAO) of the United Nations, Second Edition.

Supe, S.V. (1983). *An Introduction to Extension Education*, New Delhi, Oxford & IBH, Second Printing 1984.

Tuazon, R.R. (1991). Bridging the gap in rural extension work. *Agricultural Information Development Bulletin,* 13(4), pp. 17-18.

Walker, M. (1994). Agricultural Information System, Synergy and Development, *Journal of Extension System,* 10(2), pp. 1-15.

2

HISTORICAL ROOTS AND GROWTH OF EXTENSION

OVERVIEW

Extension work started as voluntary service by philanthropists and enlightened people to serve the needs for information and well being of ruralites. While it began as out of school education it has over the years been formalised and turned into a very systematically organised professional service. Co-operative Extension Service of USA is the first organised extension work in the world, which served as model for emulation and adaptation for various countries. In India, organised extension work was mostly post-independence phenomenon. The principles and methods of extension were imported from USA. The approach of extension in India changed from time to time from general, overall development to target group approach and training and visit extension system. Extension work has been reformed and strengthened with the help and support from the World Bank. New vistas of extension are opening-up broadening its application to different fields. Participatory approach to extension, increasing use of media and privatization of extension are some of the emerging aspects of extension.

Extension work has now become part and parcel of rural development strategy in most nations of the world. The World Bank has also contributed significantly of late, towards strengthening extension organisations in less developed nations. There is tremendous faith in extension's potentials to work with rural people. How has extension assumed such an exalted status? Like it is said that Rome was not built in a day, it was built and built, and builtextension was not master minded by one individual at a place rather it evolved through hard work of several people around the world for over more than a century now.

EARLY FORM OF EXTENSION

History of extension work is intimately related with developments in technology. The need for extension work was felt acutely in Europe and North America during early 1700s, in the wake of industrial development. It was this urge to take advances of science and technology to the door steps of farmers that agricultural societies were formed. The first such society is said to have been established in Scotland in 1728. In Europe such societies came up to spread academic knowledge of agriculture through lectures and publications (True, 1928). Thus, agricultural societies were first such bodies to undertake works which were later called extension.

The roots of extension education, however, can also be traced back to 1840s when the term university extension or extension of university was used in Britain to propose an educational innovation to take the knowledge to doorsteps of common people. The first practical steps were taken in 1867-68 when James Stuart, Fellow of Trinity College, Cambridge, England gave lectures to Women's associations and working men's clubs. Stuart is called as Father of University extension. He approached the authorities of University of Cambridge to organise extension lectures. The system was accepted by University of Cambridge in 1873 and Oxford in 1878. The work was being referred as extension movement by 1880s. (Banden Van and Hawkins, 1988).

Significant Events in USA

The first agricultural society was established in Philadelphia in 1785. Later such societies came up in other States too to spread scientific and practical knowledge of agriculture. Agricultural societies in many of the eastern States were instrumental in giving public lectures to farmers in agriculture. By 1899 forty-seven states were holding farmers' institutes using men from agricultural colleges and successful farmers. These societies later created political pressure and compelled the government to give emphasis on agricultural education.

Land Grant College

The growing pressure of people to start educational opportunities for working men in subjects of practical interest resulted in passing of Morril Act (in 1862) or Land Grant College Act. Thus, land grant colleges were established in each State. The spirit and philosophy of land grant colleges were broad enough to take education beyond the classroom for farmers and others. The land grant colleges/universities organised a number of extension activities in the form of publications and extension lectures.

Research Farms

The impetus of extension work was furthered with establishment of experiment station with each land grant college, after passing of Hatch Act of 1887. Thus, a tradition of extension work began in the form of demonstration, farmers' institutes, printed bulletin and correspondence courses in agriculture.

Dr. Seaman A. Knapp

Dr. Seaman A. Knapp is acknowledged as father of extension work in USA for his pioneering venture to set up demonstration farms through local support to show solutions to prevailing problems. Demonstration techniques were used for the first time to teach control methods to overcome insect attack in cotton.

Seed Corn Trains

Seed corn trains were organised in Iowa in 1904-5 by one Prof. Holden to reach the message of better corn seeds to large number of people through trains to widely scattered places. Widespread educational programmes through trains caught the imagination in the other states too. By 1911 there were 71 such trains in 28 states.

Youth Work

Youth clubs started around 1907 with first federally sponsored club in Mississippi. Corn growing, gardening, canning, livestock raising, etc. stimulated the interests of the youths. Educational potential of club work was recognised by early extension workers. Club for girls were also organised. Extension work later depended a lot on trained volunteers. The volunteer approach stimulated rural leadership development, which was distinguishing feature of American Extension work.

Smith Lever Act of 1914

Extension work had been started by many states prior to 1914. Smith Lever Act was the most comprehensive and well organised thinking on nation-wide activities concerning agricultural extension work. Co-operative extension service provided the mechanism for the distribution of new scientific truths. It was co-operative venture between Land-Grant Colleges – U.S. Department of Agriculture, Federal Government and people. Co-operative extension service faced emergency of World War I, (1917-1919), with characteristic efficiency, by multiplying the work force and organising intensive educational activities. The war was followed by the farm depression of the 1920s. Extension's work-force thinned and funds also shrinked. The stimulated emphasis on use of voluntary force. Extension was also responsible for organising co-operatives during this period. Major technological advances in agriculture in 1940s in the form of hybrid graln varieties, artificial insemination of cattle, chemical control of agricultural pests and new soil tillage and fertilization procedures were taken by extension organisations to the American agriculturists. However, with changes in occupational patterns as well as owing to complexity of modern living, the context and approach of programmes shifted in1960, and 1970s by expanding subject matter areas and target audience. The U.S. cooperative system has shown a lot of flexibility and adaptability to deal with a variety of problems and solutions.

Thus, extesnion which was nurtured in USA and made a professional activity, had emphasis on grassroots approach, democratic values, people's involvement, practical learning, linkage of villages with knowledge producing organisation and systematic organisational procedures. Besides, adequate attention was given to teaching of extension education. Linkage of extension with land grant university provided fertile ground for proper growth of the discipline as well. The American model of extension was adopted by many developing nations.

Thus, extension work in USA began in response to popular demand. It was strengthened by devotion and untiring efforts of volunteers, agriculturists and scholars. The co-operative extension service provided a fertile ground for giving scientific basis to organised extension work. The first ever journal of extension 'Co-operative extension service was published in USA by the professional society of the members of co-operative extension service. It helped in devising appropriate tools and techniques for enhancing effectiveness of the profession.

EXTENSION WORK IN INDIA

Organised extension work in India was started during post-independence era. Prior to independence, the alien rule under East India Company was largely concerned with maintenance of law and order rather than development. It is a historical fact that recurrent famines from 1875 to 1901 forced the colonial government to initiate agricultural research and education in the country. However, concern for villages and woes of toiling masses moved saints, sheers and social leaders to launch voluntary efforts at rural reconstruction. One can find resemblance of extension work in these endeavours of pre-independence era.

Pre-independence Efforts

Sevagram Project

Entry of Mahatma Gandhi in Indian national politics in 1919 inspired a new wave of back to the village movement Gandhi mobilised massive following while working at Wardha. Sevagram project (1920) symbolised deep personal involvement of Gandhi in translating ideal of rural development in action. Wardha later became centre for training of volunteers in Gandhian approach to rural development.

Sriniketan

Effort at rural development was initiated by legendary figure Shri Ravindra Nath Tagore at Sriniketan, West Bengal in 1921. This project, co-incidentally, had many elements of extension education in both spirit and action. Activities like demonstration on scientific methods of agriculture, training of youths, adult education and health co-operatives were important aspects of the work aimed to make a group of villages self-reliant. This was a very comprehensive programme combining culture, health, education and economic aspects of village life together. Concept of village level workers and regeneration of village organisation were put to work. The projects at Sriniketan were closely guided by Mr. Leonard Elmhirst, an Englishman, with training in agricultural economics from Cornell, USA. Thus, principles and methods of extension work are clearly evident in Sriniketan's approach of rural development.

Marthandam Project

Marthandam project launched by Young Men's Christian Association (YMCA) in 1921 under Dr. Spencer Hatch, started with the idea of establishing demonstration centres in the midst of a rural area to provide income generating activities. Dr. Hatch was again from USA with degree on Rural Sociology from Cornell.

Gurgaon Project

Gurgaon project, another exemplary effort with extension ideals, had been motivated by Mr. F.L. Bryan, an Englishman, in 1928. A village guide had been posted to act as a channel through which the advice of the experts in various departments could be passed on to the villagers. The programme of introducing improved seed, implements, the methods of cultivation, etc. were started throughout the district.

Baroda Project

Baroda Project in erstwhile princely state in Western India was initiated by enlightened ruler with the help from Spencer Hatch of YMCA. The project aimed to change outlook of farmers to motivate them to take up scientific cultivation as well as develop village leadership.

In brief, extension efforts during pre-independence era were scattered, mostly voluntary and on small areas. Spirit and to some extent procedures of extension were put to application. However, the apathy of the government and lack of financial support inhibited their growth.

Extension Efforts during Post-independence Era

Organised extension work through national government in India has passed through three distinct phases viz. extensive (Community Development and National Extension Service embraced all-round development), intensive (IADP, IAAP, HYVP) and Reformed Agricultural Extension (Training and Visit System). At present, extension work in the country is being carried out by five distinct organisation system (Mishra, 1992).

1. National Extension Service which is the main extension service, run by State Department of Agriculture, is also known as training and visit system of Agricultural Extension and co-ordinated by Ministry of Agriculture, Department of Agriculture and Co-operation at the centre.
2. The Indian Council of Agricultural Research (ICAR) and State Agricultural Universities (SAU) Extension System also carry out limited extension work.
3. The public sector undertaking extension system which includes extension by undertaking in the co-operative sector and commodity specific extension undertaken by statutory commodity boards, with no coordination among themselves or linkages with other extension

systems.

4. Private companies usually conduct product specific extension work with no coordination among themselves or with other extension systems.
5. Voluntary organisations conduct their own extension programmes with non co-ordination among themselves or with other extension systems.

Governmental Efforts

Etawah Pilot Project (1948) under Alber Mayar, an American architect, ex-soldier and rural development enthusiast introduced principles of agricultural extension in the first government-sponsored programme of rural development in Etawah, U.P. It was believed that implementation of the project would provide first hand experience of development administration, hitherto unknown in the country. The concept of multipurpose extension worker was tried for the first time. Besides, introduction of new agricultural technologies, organisation of co-operatives and programmes of health, sanitation, social education, etc., had been taken up. The programme developed village leadership and showed progress of agricultural front. Nilokheri experiment (1948) was another well known project started under leadership of Mr. S.K. Dey in order to rehabilitate the families displaced from West Pakistan due to partition. Vocational training-cum-production centre had been initiated. It was an example of success in co-operation and community work. Etawah Pilot Project and Nilokheri were small experiments with lessons for planners and policy makers.

Community Development/National Extension Service

Time was ripe by 1952 to launch nation wide programme or rural development called Community Development, adopting principles and method of extension education. It was a programme of overall development promoting all sided development of village community. With creation of National Extension service (1953), an organisational structure for carrying out development work came into being. Community development Blocks with about 100 villages in its jurisdiction were the centre of all development activities. A team of extension specialists belonging to rurally oriented disciplines under the leadership of Block development officers were appointed. Village level Extension workers were multipurpose extension agents at the grassroot level. It was for the first time in the country that the concept of development administration was translated into reality with appropriate organisational structure and personnel at Block, District, State and Central level. Extension education was chosen as means to catalyse development in all aspects of village life. The organisational infrastructure and cadre of extension personnel were the main planks of Indian approach to rural development.

Intensive Extension

The focus of rural development changed from all sided general development of C.D. to mono-purpose agricultural development within less than a decade. Intensive approach to agricultural development was the call of 1960s in order to augment agricultural production rapidly. Intensive Agricultural district programme (1960) aimed to provide inputs, credit, training and farm advice for those ready to formulate scientific farm plan. Thus, intensive extension was needed to transform traditional subsistence farming habits to one of improved agriculture. Later, new agricultural strategies were formulated and intensive Agricultural Area Programme (IAAP) as well as High Yielding Variety Programme (HYVP) helped in boosting agricultural production. The role of extension was to motivate farmers, being awareness, inculcate new skills and inspire adoption of new technologies. Thus, many supporting services were created simultaneously. The State Agricultural Universities were started in every state to generate new knowledge. Farmer's Training centres, National demonstration scheme, farm and home broadcasting on it of All India Radio and farmer's functional literacy programme were launched simultaneously during 1965-1966.

Target-Group Approach

The thrust of rural development programme in the country took sharp turn by 1970 by initiation of programmes for special group of beneficiaries and neglected regions, in order to improve the lot of small marginal farmers, landless labourers, drought prone regions, hill areas etc. Thus, Small Farmers Development Agency (SFDA), Marginal Farmers Development and Agricultural Labours agency, Drought Prone Area Programme, Hill Area Development Programme, Tribal Area Development Programmes, etc. came up in 1970. These programmes were launched through specially created institutions. However, the block level extension set up remained intact and also involved to some extent. Another about turn in approach of rural development was noticed with launching of Integrated Rural Development Programme in 1976 which was meant for the poor and oppressed group of people in rural areas to provide them income and employment. A series of schemes were launched to provide loans, subsidy and training in income generating skill and create assets so that the target group of beneficiaries can enhance their economic status. The same approach was further strengthened in 1980s and 1990s. However, the extension functionaries and approach of extension remained unchanged. There was not much thinking on this aspect.

Reorganised Agricultural Extension System

Another significant event in the history of agricultural extension work was introduction of training and visit system in the country with financial help and support from the World Bank. To start with pilot projects were started in Rajasthan and Madhya Pradesh in 1974 the positive results inspired gradual expansion of the project throughout the country. The training and visit system called for major overhaul of the existing agricultural extension system by initiating reorganisation at all levels.

The new system called for single line of command from the state headquarters to the grassroot level. The extension personnel were made responsible for professional agricultural extension works and not the other applied activities. A systematic chain of training was started from higher level (District/Zonal) down to the last ladder in order to formulate specific recommendations for the areas at particular time. Systematic visits are conducted soon after training to disseminate messages. At the grassroot level, contact farmers are selected (almost 10 per cent out of total farm families), to serve as key communicators. The village extension workers (grassroot level functionary) contact the selected farmers on their visits. There is close and constant interaction with the research system. The State Agricultural Universities and their out-reach stations do not only conduct Monthly Workshops for subject matter specialists but also take interest in research problems based on needs of the farmers. There is provision for joint visits of university scientists, and extension officers to the farmer's fields from time to time.

The reformed agricultural extension system provides for better co-ordination with development departments, people's organisation and research system. The links with input and credit agencies are carefully defined similarly an on-going process of evaluation has been built into the system. The organisational set-up of the reorganised extension system is presented below.

Field Level: A Village Extension Worker (V.E.W.) is provided for a group of 500 farm families in intensive areas like major irrigation systems or areas with large distance or having other special considerations and for a group of 800 farm families in the unirrigated areas. One Agricultural Extension Officer (AEO) is provided for 8 V.E.Ws at the block level.

Sub-divisional Level: A sub-division covering about 3-5 blocks, is the basic unit for the operation of this system. Since, the sub-division is the unit for training for the extension workers, it is supported by a team of Subject Matter Specialists (SMSs), especially in the fields of Agronomy and Plant Protection along with the Training Officer. This unit is headed by the Sub-divisional Extension Officer.

District Level : A district headed by a District Extension Officer and assisted by a team of Subject Matter Specialists covering 3-5 sub-divisions is normally the unit for implementation of programmes at this level.

Zonal Level : In case of too many districts to be supervised directly by the headquarters, one additional level has been provided, the zonal level. The Zonal Extension Officer (Z.E.O.) is responsible for all extension activities in the districts under him. In other matters, the links between the department and the districts will be through the ZEO.

State Level : The extension service is placed under a whole time Additional Director of Agriculture (Extension) with suitable technical assistance under the overall charge of the Director of Agriculture. The A.D.A. (Extension) is fully responsible for the implementation of Extension activities, in the state he is assisted by a team of most senior SMSs.

The most important gains from introduction training and visit system under National Agricultural Extension Project (NAEP) in the country include improved training capacity, better information support and enhanced research-extension linkage. Training for effective job performance of extension personnel is a must for upgrading technical, managerial and communication skills. A number of training institutions are now available for imparting training for different levels of participants as below.

In order to provide better communication support under training and visit system, capacities for preparation of information materials including print, graphics and video, have been enhanced at national and state levels. Training in communication and workshop on video production technologies as well as video equipments, offset press, Xerox copies, photo and other equipments have been provided at state headquarters and regional offices. Reorganised agricultural extension system has provided opportunities for close linkages between research, extension and farmers. There are five different levels of committees, viz. National level Research Development Co-ordination Committee, State level Technical Committees, Zonal Research Extension Advisory Committee (ZERAC), Monthly workshop and Joint Diagnostic teams. There is proposal now for District Agricultural Research and Extension implementation committee as well.

In view of the experiences gained in the country during past two decades in implementation of training and visit system, plan are afoot to broadbase existing extension services. This means that farmers should be offered advice on all their land and livestock based activities like horticulture, agroforestry, animal husbandry, etc. This means involvement of resource personnel from additional disciplines as also re-orientation of research programmes. Inclusion of more master trainers and SMSs in the needed disciplines would be required. Inclusion of women farmers and extension workers and involvement of voluntary organisation in extension for supplementing extension efforts are also being contemplated.

First Line Extension Projects of the Indian Council of Agricultural Research

The Indian Council of Agricultural Research, an apex organisation for co-ordinating agricultural research and education in the country, has a limited role in extension. It has launched a few programmes popularly known as transfer-of-technology projects or First-Line Extension Projects. The major goal behind launching these programmes is to promptly demonstrate latest agricultural technologies in the farmers' fields and gain first-hand feedback through direct interaction between scientists and farmers. It was believed that experiences gained in such sound extension programmes would help in designing model extension programmes to be implemented by general extension system. Brief description of each programme is given below.

Lab-to-Land Project (LLP)

Lab-to-Land project was launched as part of the ICAR Golden Jubilee in 1979. It aimed to bring scientists and farmers in close contact and demonstrate potentials of low-cost technologies relevant for small marginal farmers as well as landless labourers. The emphasis was made on developing farm plan, keeping in view resources available and technologies appropriate for diversification of labour use and creating supplementary sources of income.

The programme was implemented through State Agricultural Universities, ICAR Institutes, State Departments of Agriculture and Voluntary Organizations. The activities under Lab-to-Land project included creation of farm plan, and training, demonstration, field days etc. The whole programme was supposed to be used as feedback mechanism for the scientists and extension functionaries.

Krishi Vigyan Kendra (Farm Science Centre)

Krishi Vigyan Kendra (KVK) was launched in 1974 as vocational training institution for farmers and field-level extension functionaries. It aimed to impart need-based and skill-oriented training to enhance agricultural production. Training courses of each kendra should be tailored according to felt-needs and existing resources of particular area. Three fundamental principles of KVK are as follows :

(i) Agricultural production is the prime-goal.
(ii) Work experience is the main method of imparting training.
(iii) Priority of training should be on the weaker section of the society.

The KVKs are now engaged with four major functions, as given below:

(i) To organise long-term vocational training for rural youths for generating self-employment.
(ii) To organise training of farmers and extension functionaries.
(iii) To organise front-line demonstrations to generate production data and feedback.
(iv) To collaborate with subject-matter specialist of Agricultural Universities in on-farm testing, refining and documenting technologies.

KVKs are implemented through State Agricultural Universities, selected ICAR Institutes, State Government, colleges and voluntary organisations. Each KVK has been provided with about a dozen scientific staff and equal number of supporting staff, all led by Training Organiser (T.O.). The scientific staff belong to Agronomy, Agricultural Extension, Animal Science/Veterinary Science, Home Science and Plant Protection disciplines. KVKs are monitored and guided by zonal coordinating unit at the zonal level. At the central level, the division of Agricultural Extension, headed by the Deputy Director General, is responsible for overall implementation of KVK scheme. The ICAR provides guidelines and conducts periodic supervision. KVK plans and executes its activities with help and guidance from local management committees. The KVK is provided with its own building, demonstration farms, equipment, vehicles, farmers hostels staff quarters, etc. Each KVK is supposed to have 20 hectares of farm land for demonstration and practical training.

National Demonstration Project

National demonstration project was initiated in 1964-65 with a view to obtain maximum return per unit area per unit time on the cultivator's fields. It was to provide opportunity to scientists to demonstrate validity of their findings on farmer's field. NDP was implemented in selected districts through State Agricultural Universities with the help of a team of scientists, training as well as demonstrations and other extension activities. The scientists were expected to conduct different types of demonstrations as given below :

— Multiple cropping demonstration
— Rainfed cultivation demonstration
— Special problem soil demonstration
— Entire farming system demonstration

Operational Research Project

Operational Research Projects (ORPs) were initiated with a view to implement research project right in the villages in order to identify socio-economic, cultural technological and administrative constraints in a compact area. Thus, the ORPs had the whole village watershed area as target and the aim was to study operational problems in transfer of technology. The ORP had the following specific objectives :

— To test, adopt and demonstrate new agricultural technology on farmers fields in the whole village or cluster of contiguous villages/watershed area.

— To determine profitability of the new technologies and their place of spread among farmers.

— The identity and constraints both technological and socio-economic which are barrier to rapid change.

— To demonstrate group action as a method of popularising the modern technologies at a faster rate.

The ORPs were implemented through State Agricultural Universities ICAR Institutes State Departments of Agriculture and Voluntary organisations having necessary scientific background and support for rural/agricultural development. The ORPs are concerned with mixed farming, integrated, pest management, land reclamation, post-harvest technology, plantation, crops, fisheries, land management etc.

Technology Assessment and Refinement through Institution Village Linkage Programme (IVLP)

Technology Assessment and refinement through Institution Village Linkage Programme (IVLP) is one of the recent programmes of the ICAR emphasizing on technology integration. The technology integration in contrast to technology transfer, refers to the process or a set of activities that must happen if a new scientific agricultural information is put to use in any farm production system. In view of three districts types of agriculture, viz. commercial green revolution and complex, diverse and risk prone (CDR), there is need for technological intervention through technology assessment and refinement with the emphasis on stability and sustainability for small production system, maintaining productivity and profitability with environmental concerns for well defined farm production systems and appropriate for value addition in case of commercial farm production system. Thus, IVLP is a programme for generating appropriate technologies by refining and assessing innovation generated by scientists knowledgeable about their respective disciplines. However, various factors operating in the farm production system of small farmers hitherto not considered by scientists, affect adoption process. IVLP, therefore, has following specific objectives :

(i) To introduce technological intervention with emphasis on stability and sustainability alongwith productivity of small production systems.

(ii) To introduce and integrate the appropriate technologies to sustain technological interventions and their integration to maintain productivity and profitability taking environmental issues into considerations in a comparatively well defined production system.
(iii) To introduce and integrate the appropriate technologies to increase the agricultural productivity with marketable surplus in commercial farm production systems.
(iv) To facilitate adoption of appropriate post-harvest technologies for conservation and on-farm value addition of agricultural products, by-products and wastes for greater economic dividend and national priorities.
(v) To facilitate adoption of appropriate technologies for removal of drudgery, increased efficiency and higher income of farm women.
(vi) To monitor socio-economic impact of the technological intervention for different production systems.
(vii) To identify extrapolation domains for new technology/technology modules based on environmental characterization at meso and mega levels.

The IVLP is being implemented through ICAR institute headquarters, SAU Headquarters, Regional Research Stations/Zonal Research Stations of the ICAR Institutes and SAUs and KVKs. The centres selected for the purpose have required infrastructural facilities, viz. in terms of team of scientists, laboratory, transport, etc. Each centre has to adopt a village or clustre of villages representing the district.

Role of State Agricultural Universities in Extension

State Agricultural Universities (SAUs) were set up in India on the pattern of Land Grant Universities of U.S.A. with integrated teaching, research and extension functions. Each SAU was expected to perform some extension roles in the area under its jurisdiction. However, extension role of SAU was supposed to be complementary to the major extension efforts made by State Department of Agriculture. The specific extension roles of SAUs are as given below (Anon., 1974).

(i) To prepare personnel to perform various extension roles and provide dynamic and analytic leadership to extension programmes through a sound, systematic and integrated under-graduate and post-graduate teaching in extension education

(ii) To collect, process and disseminate latest research findings to extension personnel and extension clientele through appropriate methods and media.

(iii) To identify field problems to which scientific solutions are not yet available and communicate these to the concerned subject matter departments.

(iv) To produce information materials and teaching aids for extension personnel, trainers and farmers.

(v) To plan, organise and conduct production and problem oriented training of various types and duration for extension personnel, farmers and others concerned with development programmes.

(vi) To provide authentic and systematic guidance through an uptodate and specialised 'Farm and Home Advisory Service' to farmers, farm women, farm youth, extension personnel, bankers, input dealers, manufacturers, voluntary farm organisations and others concerned with agricultural development.

(vii) To undertake researches on various facets of extension education with a view to enriching programme formulation and operation, and gaining insight into the process of dynamics of planned change.

(viii) To undertake adaptive and operational research projects with a view to testing applicability of findings under different soil, agro-climatic and socio-economic conditions in the different parts of the state.

In order to perform these roles each SAU has a fullfledged Directorate of Extension with following major units.

Farm Advisory Service

Extension workers and farmers need advice on technical matters such advice should be readily available with the help of concerned subject matter specialists.

Training

Training of farmers, farm women, youth and extension personnel has become one of the major responsibilities of SAUs and appropriate infrastructure have been created for the purpose.

Communication of Information

Collection, processing and dissemination of latest research findings to extension personnel and extension clientele through appropriate methods and media are done through communication centres in many SAUs. Besides, information materials and teaching aids need to be provided to extension personnel and teachers. Thus, communication unit has production, service and information communication roles to play.

Field Extension

Each SAU undertakes field extension programmes in the areas under its jurisdiction through subject matter specialists of Directorate of Extension or regional stations. Besides the transfer of technology programmes of ICAR viz. National Demonstration, KVK, LLP, ORP and Technology Assessment and Refinement through Institutional Village Linkage Programme (IVLP) are also implemented. Some SAUs have well planned field extension programmes of their own.

Extension Role of Voluntary Organisations

Voluntarism is derived from latin word *'Voluntas'* which means will. The free will assumes various forms of impulses, passions and desire to act. The term 'volunteer' is normally used to denote someone who offers unpaid service to a good cause. There are many sources of motivation behind voluntarism like religion, love of mankind, or mutual aid. Voluntary organisation refers to non-profit organisations set up by a group of persons on voluntary basis to help people of a locality in self-reliant development in order to satisfy their needs.

Voluntary organisations must be representatives of the needs and aspirations of the people and should not expect to get in return for the services rendered. It must also be free from external control. People's involvement in all the activities is essential. Ideally the emphasis should be on raising consciousness of the people and strengthening their capacities to solve their own problems. Voluntary organisations are most sought after for developmental due to their unique features as given below :

(i) Voluntary organisations exhibit high level of commitment for the cause.
(ii) There is a sense of innovativeness or eagerness to experiment with

ideas and solve the problems.

(iii) Voluntary workers are enthusiastic about the work and pursue it unto their last because of high level of motivation.

(iv) The organisations are usually free of complex procedure and can adapt their rules to suit local conditions.

(v) There is concern for humanity and its all-round development. Thus, the programmes are comprehensive.

(vi) As voluntary organisations are initiated by local people or those having concern, there is close contact with people.

Trends in Growth of V.O.'s in Rural Development in India

India has a long tradition of voluntary action through a system of '*dharma*' (obligation) and '*daan*' (charity). That explains the proliferation of trusts, temples charity organisation, etc. from long back in past. However, during pre-independence era specially in the late nineteenth century there was uprise in national movement. Fired by modern thinking and dynamic enthusiasm, the leaders and reformers lead organisations with ideas of co-operation, nationalism. Village self-government and village self sufficiency was actively canvassed by the Gandhian Institutions. No doubt, the post-independence emphasis on community organisation was influenced by the guidelines of the First Five Year Plan. Voluntary organisations had been identified by the government as social organisations. There had been quite some effort to attract them.

The continuous visitation of calamities in the country helped in proliferation of V.O.'s engaged in relief activities. There was phenomenal increase in the scale of foreign funding and entry of V.O.'s from abroad. International support and contributions were available in form of food grains, milk powder, medical supplies drilling rigs, etc. Looking to the sudden increase in foreign funding and entry of foreigners in the isolated rural areas, the government wished to avoid the unintended consequences. Thus, it was decided that money coming from abroad must be classified properly. The government decided to get money from abroad through Freedom From Hunger Campaign Office in the Ministry of Agriculture. Later an organisation called People's Action for Development, India was set up as official agency with non-official representation. It advocated a certain self-reliant approach of development through mobilisation of community resources. The trend changed from relief to development with eye on permanence.

Legal Criteria for Voluntary Organisation

In view of the increasing participation of voluntary organisations in rural development, the Seventh Plan document of the Government of India has laid down following criteria for identifying voluntary organisations and enlisting them for help in relation to rural development.

(i) It must be a registered society under the Registration of Societies Act, 1860.
(ii) It must be based in rural area and should have worked there for a minimum of three years.
(iii) It should have broad based objectives serving the social and economic needs of the community as a whole and the weaker section in particular. It should not work for profit but on 'no-profit and no-loss basis'.
(iv) Its activities should be open to all citizens of India, irrespective of religion, caste, creed, sex or race.
(v) It should have the necessary flexibility, professional competence and organisational skills to implement programmes.
(vi) Its office bearers should not be elected members of any party.
(vii) It must declare that it will adopt constitutional and non-violent means for rural development purposes.
(viii) It must be committed to secular and democratic concepts and methods of functioning.

The Lacunae of V.Os

There is surfeit of voluntary organisations lured by increasing of recognition, money, power or clout over people. It is increasingly becoming difficult to identify the genuine ones. Some of the prominent limitations are as follows :

(i) The dominance of powerful personality as head of organisation in order to serve vested interests kills the very spirit of voluntarism. Often, there is lack of freedom among workers to carry out works and help the needy.
(ii) In the name of ideals, religion or superior cause, there is systematic exploitation of young unemployed people by paying them meagre salaries and using them to serve some ulterior motives.
(iii) The programmes implemented are by and large agency oriented rather

than on the basis of felt needs of the people.

(iv) There is over-dependence on funding agencies and government. Thus, there is indirect control of the donors and bureaucracy on the programmes.

(v) Many organisations due to their religious, political or economic ideologies alienate people for partisan interests. They propagate messages not compatible with peace and harmony of different ethnic groups.

(vi) Very few voluntary organisations operate at the grass-roots level with the people and take the burden of confronting with the powers that be. A bulk of them are engaged in providing services or supplies or implementation of programmes funded by the government.

(vii) Recruitment, training and retention of committed worker is far from satisfactory in majority of cases. Professionalisation of voluntary service demand action in this regard.

(viii) No doubt, the methodology of working and creating self-reliant society must also be rational and progressive without creating undue dependence on outside sources. There is little concern for permanence, development of local leadership and sustainability issues in development approach of the V.Os.

(ix) The arrival of increasing number of voluntary organisations, emergence of their federations and associations may breed a politics of different kind. It may be used by the power hungry.

The Merits of V.Os.

The number of voluntary organisations is continuously on the rise. There are divergent views about the significance of voluntary organizations. The government recognised the value of V.Os. for entrusting them with the responsibilities of implementing certain programmes of rural development. It is now evident that the government organisations have certain limitations in complementing rural development programmes with the spirit of service and dedication. Paid, career-oriented personnel cannot be forced to work with emotions and attachments nor can the rules be stretched all on a sudden. Hence, keeping the strengths and weaknesses of government organisations in perspective, voluntary organisations have a definite role to play. They are in no way competing with each other, rather V.Os. will supplement the government agencies in many ways. Some of the functional areas suitable for intervention of V.Os. are given below :

Information Dissemination : The government programmes need to be communicated to the people in their language and from the people's perspectives. This task is often left to the lower level functionaries of the government. All the efforts of publicity through various media do not always reach the intended beneficiaries. Information is power and V.Os. can strengthen people with right information to one and all. In the similar way, genuine feedback about the benefits and reactions of people can be fed forward to the planner.

Community Organisation and Mobilisation : Due to close contact of V.Os. with the people, it is possible for them to organise self-help groups in the communities. They can generate local leadership and collect funds for common facilities. In fact, V.Os. are quite capable to play catalytic role in mobilisation of community to set up its own facilities and solve their own problems.

Utilisation of Local Resources : Identification, planning and effective use of local resources, skills and knowledge can help rural areas in big way. Unutilized resources can be turned into profitable enterprise through appropriate training and enterprise.

To Set Ideals of Development Work : V.Os. can show through their organisation works and technique live examples. V.Os. may like to concentrate their work on appropriate technology, team work and ways of living, which people can emulate by seeing. The permanent changes can be brought through such ideal work.

Conscientisation of the Poor : It is a common knowledge that no development can be brought unless people themselves begin to realize the problem. Such realization requires efforts to break the shackles of ignorance and vicious cycle of exploitation. It is here that V.Os. can play significant role. It requires confrontation with reality and powerful forces. It may upset the power structure of community. Thus, only genuinely committed V.Os. can dare to venture in this work.

NEW DIRECTIONS IN EXTENSION WORK

Extension work is undergoing a phase of transition due to various factors such as technological innovations, developments in media, changes in organisations and perception about development itself.

Thus, many new trends are emerging such as inclusion of new subject matter areas, in the fold of extension education, privatisation, media use, participatory methods of extension work, farmers network, etc., as enumerated below.

New Subject Matter Areas

Extension though started with improvement in agriculture and home economics in early years, it soon embraced other subject matter areas concerning rural living viz. fisheries, forestry, livestock, veterinary, dairy etc. However, with changing demography in the developed nations, a bulk of population in Europe and North America is urban. Extension in many of these countries is now focussing on new subject-matter areas of relevance to the majority viz. environment, energy, preventive healthcare, consumer education, natural resources management, etc. With success of extension in public education, many democratically elected governments find it natural to propagate public awareness about many new areas like family welfare, teen-age pregnancy, drug prevention, care of the elderly through time tested methods of extension education. The World Bank supported extension is broadening its narrow focus from crops to livestock, land use, water-management, conservation of natural resource in order to provide much needed technological support to farmers.

Privatisation of Extension

Extension is increasingly being seen as a profitable resource having commercial value. Thus, there is growing tendency in developed nations towards making agricultural extension into a profitable enterprise. It is believed that clients should pay partially to fully for self financing of extension work. With resource crunch and financial crisis being encountered by many national governments, there is probably need to generate funds. Many large scale farmers and agribusiness organisations can willingly pay for the advice and assistance received from extension organisations. In Britain, the main goal of its extension service is to be leading consultancy to farmers and agribusiness to provide quality service. Of late, Government of Rajasthan State of India has decided to involve private sector voluntary agency to undertake extension at the grassroot level and gradually minimise government's role in extension work. This new trend is giving rise to misperception that public-funded extension service is biased towards those who can afford the high price. With increasing emphasis on profit, the attention would now turn to physically well endowed regions, cash crops and big farmers. Further, the public organisation would be weakened in comparison to private organisation.

Media Use

Agricultural extension, for long, has depended on traditional modes of communication, mostly face-to-face contacts with individuals and groups despite the fact that number of extension workers is woefully inadequate in many parts of the world. Many experts feel that traditional extension is labour intensive and not well-equipped to meet diverse information needs to all categories of farmers. (Modi, 1992). Communication media, offer a lot of advantages for reaching messages to masses more precisely and quickly. Above all, range of communication media has expanded far beyond imagination. There are exciting new features available in the new communication technologies combining both capacity of broadcast and miniaturization of equipments in order to facilitate grassroot level production and distribution. Availability of computer and telecommunication facilities are opening new vistas of communication. According to Antholt (1992) there is little argument about potential cost effectiveness of modern communication technologies. There is also a wide body of experiences to suggest that extension has not been effective in reaching these potentials.

Participatory Approaches to Extension

Extension work being carried out by bureaucratic government organisations under rigid rules.is seen as anti-thesis of human emphasis on people-oriented extension organisations at the grassroots with emphasis on effective use of community's resources. The knowledge and experiences of people should be the starting point to solve community's problems. Farmers are being viewed as active partners in development of innovations and their dissemination in the community. Farming systems Research and Extension, Participatory Technology Development and Farmer First extension are new waves of extension calling for active roles of farmers and building structures for farmer to farmer extension. Extension in the changed scenario is more farmer-propelled and interactive.

NETWORKING FARMERS

There is urgent present need to devise structures to link farmers with similar concerns and mission together in search of solutions of their problems. Networks can provide such forum to people with common vision, and need to maintain contact. This is more relevant for self-reliance of farmers, specially to those not having ready access to extension advice. They can use their network to gather needed information. However, there are a number of questions to be answered before thinking about formation of farmers networks, as given below :

(i) Are there common problems faced and realized by potential members?
(ii) Are there relevant experiences/stocks of knowledge to be shared?
(iii) Do members have good idea of what a network is and how could they use it?
(iv) Are they prepared to spend time and energy in sharing and networking.
(v) Is there atmosphere of openness to share mistakes and learn from each other.

Functions of Farmers Networks

A number of possible activities can be undertaken by farmers network, as given below :

(i) Make contact with outside agencies donor organisations, etc.
(ii) Study and document existing agricultural practices which are economically viable.
(iii) Increase interaction between farmers and encourage exchanges through, tours, meetings, newsletters, etc.
(iv) Apply gathered stock of knowledge and skills to solve problem.
(v) Evaluate implications of technologies or government policies affecting their vocation.
(vi) Advisory function to others interested.
(vii) Form alternative solutions and programmes of development.

Organising Network

It requires some baseline survey to determine the need of potential member and extent of commitment to work together for cause. Depending upon the objectives formal or semiformal structure need to be created. A steering committee or administrative body should be formed to pull fund, distribute responsibilities and carry out functions.

In India, a network of small and marginal farmers interested in LEISA (Low External Input SustainableAgriculture) was formed in Tamil Nadu and Pondicherry in 1990. Farmers depending on rainfed agriculture and livestock decided to search alternatives to unsustainable land use practices such as massive deforestation and use of chemicals and other expensive inputs. The organisation for network was initiated through a regional workshop of farmers with common interest. It has now a formal structure with central secretariat, personnel and range of activities, viz. documentation, meetings, workshops, seminars, tours, newsletter, publications, etc. (ILIEA, 1992).

Lessons learnt from experiences of farmers network in developing nations indicate that, initially an informal organisational structure with focus on actions are perceived as important by members. Then autonomy of members and their representation should be considered. Type of activities chosen for the network should be within limits of time and energy so as to allow for frequent meetings and sharing.

EXTENSION IN GENERAL UNIVERSITIES

Extension has now become part and parcel of agricultural higher education in India. General universities had so far been concentrating on teaching and research alone, confining their activities within four walls. With initiatives of pioneering thinkers and policy makers, extension has now become third and important dimension fo general education. There are 95 universities having departments/centres of adult, continuing education and extension (ACEE) spread all over the country. Though all the departments, centres have not taken up activities equally intensively, some beginning has already been made. There is a general fear and hitch among the educated elites about content and manner of contact with the masses. However, there is no dearth of subject-matter areas to be covered under extension programmes.

Extension seeks to disseminate knowledge for the benefit of community. Thus, concepts of home science, environment, commerce, botany, economics and management, law, sociology, social work, etc. can be directly used to address to the information needs of the people. However, there is need to orient the teachers about their extension roles and nature of activities to be undertaken by the ACEE Units (Vaishampayan, 1996).

REFERENCES

Anonymous (1978). Report of the Review Committee on Agricultural Universities, ICAR, New Delhi, June 1978.

True, A.C. (1928). A History of agricultural extension in the United States In *Yearbook of the U.S. Department of Agriculture,* 1989 (pp. 157-190), Washington D.C., U.S. Government Printing Press Office.

Ban, A.W. Vanden and Hawkins, H.S. (1988). *Agricultural Extension,* Longman Scientifc & Technical Pub., U.K.

3

COMMUNICATION SUPPORT IN EXTENSION WORK

OVERVIEW

Extension uses communication as tool to bring about positive changes in rural communities. Communication is more than just transfer of information. It is sharing of meaning, calling for two-way communication. Such audience-based participatory communication approach has been termed as 'Development Communication'. There are range of different methods and media available today from farm and home visit to demonstration field trip, radio, television, etc. Indigenous channels and new communication technologies also count. However, extension work must use well planned communication strategy to bring the desired effects.

Extension work has rightly been labelled as communication intervention. Extension workers use a variety of methods and media of communication. However, experiences all over the world suggested that there is need to improve communication dimension of extension work so that there is more interaction with the people. This chapter aims to describe meaning and role of communication, types of communication, commonly used methods and media of communication and steps in formulation of communication strategy.

WHAT IS COMMUNICATION?

Communication is a popular term. When a person gives good public speech we call him a good communicator. If two people are talking, we say that they are communicating. Many people refer to various media of communication; viz. radio, film or television as communication. None of these is true. Communication has a Latin root '*Communis*' which means common. It also requires a degree of commonness between individuals for communication to occur. The purpose of communication is to establish commonness. Communication, thus, refers to the process of sharing information, feelings or ideas in a manner that there is common understanding of meaning, intent and use of the message.

Communication is 'sharing together'. Communication is not a unit act or event. One does not begin or stop the act by speaking or writing. It gives rise to a chain in reactions. A skilful communicator anticipates reactions and observes them, so as to decide on his next approach. Thus, communication moves back and forth like a game of ball. The sender of message or communicator also becomes the receiver as he watches the reactions of audience in face to face situation. In a series of communication both sender and receiver alternate roles. Continuous exchange of information or dialogue helps in correcting misconceptions and keeping both sender and receiver tuned together. Thus, true communication can happen only if both parties are active. The receiver is not an empty container or inert material to be influenced unilaterally. All human communication requires two-way communication. Some of the distinguishing features of communication are given below :

Communication is Purposive in Nature

Need to express one's ideas and feelings is universal. All living beings crave to express. Animals and birds make different sounds to indicate their needs. Dogs bark bitterly at the sight of strangers to warn their masters. Many animals indicate warning of calamities by crying or running around restlessly. Human communication is very purposive and pre-designed. Humanbeings are intelligent enough to invent languages and other symbols to express themselves. Purpose of human communication is basically to bring commonness. It is a common to find large display boards advertising products. They are trying to influence consumer's choices by tempting them to buy the product. A political leader gives fiery speech to attract audiences. A salesman tries various ways to attract customers. Extension workers communicate information about technology so that farmers can understand, accept and act upon. Communication helps in everyday life to inform, instruct influence or entertain. There is a whole lot of industry thriving on communication for profits viz. advertisements, newspapers, magazines, television, cinema, information kiosk complete with phone, fax, computer, printer etc.

Communication can occur in many ways

Communication can happen in a number of ways as given below :

Symbolic Communication
Human beings often communicate through symbols. Red cross signifies medical practice, inverted red triangle stands for 'family planning'. Mathematical symbols +, -, × or ÷ stand for addition, subtraction, multiplication and division. While some symbols are universal, most others are culture-specific.

Body Language
The use of limbs or parts of body can also communicate ideas. Gestures for calling people and expressing thirst are common. In many cultures people find it abusive to use index finger towards someone. Similarly, pointing out leg towards someone is taken as offensive. Human beings have varieties of ways to greet and express love, hate, agreement or disagreement. Movement of eyes and facial expressions communicate intention or feelings.

Self-communication
This is a kind of communication in which everyone is engaged most of the times. Such communication within one self taken place internally on continuous basis. Here a person acts both as sender and receiver.

Communication through Physical Touch
Touching parts of body is very potent means of communication. It not only conveys facts but also feelings. Warmth of feeling, coldness or alienation can be gauged through touch. Patting part of body or shaking hand convey meaning.

Communication through Language of Silence, Colour and Space
It is said that silence is more powerful than speech. If two people are together but do not utter a single word, it surely communicates something. They are strangers or they are angry or deaf and dumb. Silence is taken as humility and sign of agreement in many cultures. Thus, silence also communicates. Many skilful communicators use silence to press their views or force decisions or express disagreement.

Colours have important role in communicating moods and feelings. hile colour conveys peace, purity and chastity. Red communicates aggressiveness, sex and vigour. Blue, green and grey are cool colours. However, colours are interpreted differently in different cultures. Colour are used to convey inner feelings.

Space also conveys some meaning. Distance between people, arrangement of space in house, office or public meeting, also communicates something. The close relationships are reflected in proximity between people in terms of space. People of different status or positions stand or sit apart. Arrangements in room also indicate formality or informality.

The timing of events or time one takes to react or complete a work also conveys intentions. Similarly time one takes to respond to a question, means something.

Media-based Communication

No communication is possible without use of five sense organs, viz. eyes (visual), ears (audio), nose (smell), taste buds (taste) or physical touch. However, use of media accelerates the effect by reinforcing desired ideas. A range of communication media are available today to use one or all of these senses in different situations.

ROLE OF COMMUNICATION IN DEVELOPMENT

Development means positive changes in socio-economic and cultural lives of majority of people on permanent basis without exploitation or violence. Rural development in most parts of the world calls for intensive efforts to tackle problems of mass illiteracy, population, malnutrition, poor health, hunger, pollution, etc. How can communication help in rural development? Communication cannot provide finance, inputs or infrastructure. But it can help in creating awareness about technologies and mobilise people to use them. Links can be created between government agencies and people as well as people to people. It is a common understanding that communication helps to inform, motivate educate and entertain. Besides it can also help in training of people, organising community forums and co-ordinating various activities, as discussed below.

Information

Information is power. Rural people need different types of information about new techniques, services, supplies and government programme

Communication can help in speedy access to needed information at grassroot level in understandable form. This can be done through radio, television, magazines, newspaper or rural information centres.

Motivation

People may not always have positive opinion to accept change or initiate action for development. The existing situations and problems need to be analysed to help them realize problems. It requires persuasive communication to convince people to try new ways or organise themselves to solve their problems. Messages to inspire people, clarify doubts and suggest new practices must be designed effectively. Such communication requires deeper understanding of people, their culture and reasons for existing situation, etc.

Education/Training

People need new knowledge, values and skills to perform better. Continuous efforts are needed to create conducive environment for informal, non-formal learning. Local language, traditional sources of information and existing way of acquiring new information should be used.

Entertainment/Cultural Enrichment

Rural people need healthy entertainment. Folk songs, dramas, stories and music help in transmission of rich cultural heritage. People need to identify their cultural roots and draw inspiration for development. Communication media can also make use of local talents and experiences.

Co-ordination

A number of organisations are engaged in the task of development. However, these organisations may not have linkage between themselves. Even one section of an organisation may not know the activities or programmes of the other. This creates duplication of efforts and confusions in the minds of people. Communication links different parts of an organisation and people to facilitate smooth implementation of development activities. There is need to communicate information about all aspects of programme to different partners.

Feedback

There is need for continuous feedback on how the programme is unfolding. Different reaction cases and concerns of the people should reach those responsible. Audio-visual documentation can also help to take remedial action.

Extension work is intricately concerned with analysing rural problems, providing information. Organising people's groups and getting feedback. Hence, communication based support is essential during planning, execution and follow-up to extension programme with increasing availability of communication media and their educational value. It is now pertinent to plan effective utilization of media. There is a recent new trend to label use of communication in development as Development Communication, as detailed below.

DEVELOPMENT COMMUNICATION

The significant contributions of communication in bringing socio-economic charges have been amply proved. However, communication is not a process of transferring information alone through media from the government to people. Development in rural areas calls for systemic use of principles of communication taking characteristics, capacities and environment of people in full view. Users must become active partners in communication. Such communication has been labelled as development communication. It is a circular process where the users are seen as active participants in the communication process and affecting the outcome of communication. It is periodically renewed by continuous evaluation. The accent of development communication is not on dissemination of information but on its reception and utilization by the users (Quebral, 1983).

Development communication in this sense must have certain essential features, as given below :

1. It is purposive and the intenTion here is to help in socio-economic development.
2. It is based on study of audience's characteristics and environment.
3. It views people not as independent atoms but as being connected to each other in networks where a good many decisions are made by cluster of individuals. Many communication strategies at village

level based on this premise.

4. It aims at educating people not simply passing along information to them.
5. It takes into account a variety of media forms, both human and non-human and mass media. An appropriate combination of mass media and inter-personal communication channel is considered more prudent. Use of localised medium with control in the hands of users seem quite befitting as in local radio, local television, community based cable TV network etc.
6. Formative (during the process of production of communication materials and summative evaluation are a must to gain constructive feedback about effectiveness of communications.

Thus, Development Communication is not publicity *per se*. It is not one way communication from those who have information to those who are ignorant. It assumes that people who face the problems do have innate capability to find solution if they are given opportunity to use their wisdom and creativity. This approach sees motivation as key element in dealing with rural audiences. It builds dialogue between people and development agencies. Balit (1988) pointed out that Development Communication is now seen as a social process designed to seek a common understanding or consensus among all the participants of development leading to concerted action. The media are now seen as useful tools to bring about this process and assist in learning. Their use is not an end in itself and inter-personal communication plays an important role too. It is quite in keeping with the goals of extension education to use development communication approach to create dialogue in order to motivate and educate rural clientele.

TYPES OF COMMUNICATION

Communication can be categorized as inter-personal group or mass communication on the basis of side of audience involved in the process. Each of this type has been described below :

Inter-personal Communication

Inter-personal communication refers to face to face communication between two people. The flow of message is between one to one person or between one to few as in conversation or dialogue. It is personal, direct and intimate. Feedback is almost immediate. Good interpersonal communication calls for understanding about individual and group psychology, empathy and group dynamics. It requires listening skills and sensitivity to the needs and views of others.

Group communication means exchanging ideas, information and skills with more than two or a group of people like in group meeting and method demonstration. Group communication is direct and personal like in interpersonal communication. But with increasing number of participants degree of participation and feedback gets lesser. There are an array of media helpful in group situation such as video, audio cassette tape, puppet show, etc.

Mass communication refers to the significant advances in communication technology by means of which message can be sent to large audience viz. Radio, T.V., Satellite communication. Mass media are only instrument and a part of the larger phenomenon called mass communication. Thus, mass communication refers to sharing of information with many people in many places with the help of machines. It indicates a kind of social communication involving distinct characteristics, as below :

Nature of Audience

Mass communication is directed toward large heterogeneous and anonymous audience. Large audience consists of too many people for the communication to interact personally during a reasonable period of time. Mass audience is heterogeneous in the sense that audience are widely dispersed, varying in occupation, age and backgrounds. The aim is to reach most audience simultaneously. Eventhough the audiences have their relationships and interactions, communicators do not know them personally.

Nature of Mass Communication Organization

These are complex and socially institutionalized form of organizations characterised by mass production and mass distributions. The roles of such institutions are linked with overall aims and objectives of larger society. A large number of personnel are engaged to carry out the complex processes.

Lack of Direct Feedback

Most mass media lack direct contact with public except for occasional letters from audience.

Mass Impact

The impact of themes and images communicated through mass media have such impact on the minds of the public that distant objects become topics of household discussion and occupy lives of the people. They create languages, heroes, stories, etc. which become shared context for many. Thus, the community or we feeling extends beyond limited confines of geography.

With decentralization of mass media and arrival of local radio and local Television Stations, there are ample of opportunities to focus on local problem. Mass media can provide attention on development programmes, mobilize people and give them opportunities to express reactions. They can inform people about needs and problems, innovation and results. New developments in technologies have provided facility of interactions in mass media also.

METHOD AND MEDIA OF COMMUNICATION

There are an array of methods and media available today. An attempt has been made here to discuss commonly available methods and media in terms of their application to extension work.

Farm and Home Visit

This is a method of direct face to face contact between farmers and extension workers at farmer's farm or home. This method is specially suited to build acquaintance with farmers and gain understanding of the problems. It is helpful to share information and teaching skills. The method brings quick results in traditional areas where farmers had not been exposed to new technologies so far.

Procedure for conducting Effective Visits

Farm and home visits are most common. In order to enhance the effectiveness, extension workers must do some advance planning, as given below:

Community Map

At the outset extension worker should obtain maps of the villages under his jurisdiction and magnify them suitably to show farm families, route to visit, etc. This can be effective visual tool to chalk out plans of visit, write reports on areas covered and works to be done.

Schedule of Visit

It is better to maintain regularity in visit if this method is to be used. Farmers should know beforehand when the extension workers will be available for advice, inspection of demonstration, discussion or any other purpose. There may be many reasons for visit to the village. Apart from normal technical advice, an extension worker may visit to conduct meeting or select beneficiary of a programme, offer help in procuring inputs or teach a new skill. Thus, an extension worker must have his activity schedule drawn. Then it is easier to focus the visit on particular objectives.

People to be visited

Who should be visited? In fact, there are many people in the communities. An extension worker must identify people who are interested to listen and try out new ideas, those with leadership skills and those who resist changes. It is better to visit variety of people. However, some target is essential to use time effectively. Experts criticise that extension workers should not always focus on large, progressive farmers. Problem of poor, marginal and less than average farmers should also be recognized.

Visits

It is better to nave system of documentation to note down the transactions made during the visits. Such records serve as easy aid to recall what happened with whom during last visit and plan further. Besides, at the end of considerable period, effects of such visits can be gauged.

It takes time and effort to build relationship. One should be patient with human interactions. Those extension workers functioning in villages different than their own native places or cultures, need to be alert to the norms, values and practices prevalent in the villages. They should acquaint themselves with local dialects and norms of behaviour. Proper greetings, respectful conversation and expression of gratefulness as prevalent in local area should be emulated. It must be remembered by every extension worker that people who work as change agents are not out there to make friends. It is a responsibility of educative kind and thus a conscious efforts is needed. Some ground rules necessary for smooth interpersonal interactions are suggested below :

— Make visits pleasant through courtesy, smooth conversation and whatever help you can offer.
— Observe local customs in greetings and making conversation.

— Let the farmers talk. Listen patiently and carefully.
— Observe farmers' crops, cattle and surroundings
— Talk in terms of farmers interest.
— Use natural and easy language.
— Be accurate in statement.
— Do not land into arguments with farmers.
— Render any other services you can readily provide in terms of contacts, literature or physical labour within your convenience.
— Carry leaflets, samples, etc. for the farmers
— End your visit in time
— Thank the farmer for the courtesies and note down if any promise is made for the next visit.
— Record the visit in terms of accomplishments, promises made, problems observed, proposed date of next visit, etc.

Advantages
— This method helps in building personal relations.
— It is useful in locating leaders.
— It is quite effective method to organise and prepare people for change.
— It is possible to contact those not participating in the programme and inspire them.
— It builds trust between extension workers, his organisation and farmers.
— It helps to get farmers' reactions about extension programmes.

Limitations
— It takes a lot of time
— It is difficult to always choose a time most convenient to the farmers.
— It is costly method
— The visit is mostly concentrated on more responsive farmers

Office Call

It is a call made by a farmer or a group of farmers on the extension worker at his office. It is not quite common method in our country. However, it can now be used in many progressive areas. Office call is most appropriate when clients are motivated. It is very economic on time and resources of extension workers.

What are the Objectives/Purposes?

— It helps in giving quick solution to farmers problems
— It facilitates timely arrangement of supplies and services
— It promotes close contact between farmers and extension organisation.
— It enables farmers to bring samples of diseased plants, insects etc.
— Extension workers can support farmers with extension literature.

Procedure for making Office Call effective

There are many opportunities now to use this method in research and extension organisations like National Agricultural Research Project (NARP), Krishi Vigyan Kendra (KVK), Krishi Gyan Kendra (KGK) etc., where scientists of different disciplines are available. Office call requires arrangement of office-space, extension literature, case files, bulletin board, etc. for effective use, as detailed below.

— Extension office should be placed at convenient location. Suitable signs should be placed outside the building, inside the building and at the entrance of office room to help the visitors in locating.
— Regular office-hours should be announced and maintained. In case of unavailability, someone should receive the visitors and record their problems.
— Office should be neat; orderly and attractive. This requires systematic organisation of space for visiting room, waiting lounge, secretarial assistance and display/bulletin boards. Arrangement for lighting, furniture and equipments should be made as per need. The convenience of the visitor and work should be considered in organising office space. Extension literature like magazines may be kept in visiting room for ready reference. Some literature may also be kept for distribution. Bulletin boards may be good tool for providing up-to-date and useful information. Provision for display of samples, specimens, photographs and models can be of help.
— In order to provide effective advice, some system of recording can be initiated so that basic information on the clients are available for future advice. Files may be opened and arranged alphabetically or village-wise.
— Extension workers may keep addresses, phone numbers and facilities available with various concerned organisations and people for ready reference. This will enhance their efficiency in dealing with farmers' problems.

The method is quite good for providing advice on problems that require detailed technical information like starting a poultry/dairy farm, installing a pump, crop planning, etc. There is good opportunity now in view of economic liberalization to use this method in progressive areas.

Advantages

— It may enhance reputation or extension worker in the community.
— It can help to identify problems of the areas.
— It is good indicator of the confidence reposed by the community in extension.

Limitations

— Extension workers cannot always be available.
— Callers may feel dissatisfied if not received or well attended in absence of extension agent.

Demonstration

This is one of the oldest extension methods, equally applicable in many different situations to build confidence of people in new ideas and persuade them to try by showing. Demonstration means to show. Demonstration should not be confused with experiment (trying new ideas under artificial conditions). Demonstration is showing proven techniques to reveal the procedure of doing or value of it. Simply speaking demonstration is a way of showing method (method demonstration) or result of a practice (result demonstration). However, there are differences between method and result demonstration as given below.

Method demonstration	*Result demonstration*
It shows how to use a practice	It show the end result/outcome
It is quite appropriate to show working of new instrument or skills in a practice	Result of a practice or product can be shown
It takes less time	It is time taking, involving all the steps to get results
No comparison is required	Comparison with old practice is essential

Advantages of demonstration

— It is very effective in stimulating learning by involving most senses.
— It makes each step easy to understand
— It can conveniently make use of other audio-visual aids like charts, posters and also combine with meetings, exhibitions, question-answer session, etc.
— It makes people convinced
— Demonstration has good publicity value. Thus, reports on demonstration can find place in newspapers or magazines and multiply its effects. It encourages people to try new practices.

Method Demonstration

It is mostly how-to-do type of demonstration following step-by-step procedures.

Planning for demonstration

1. One must choose the subject of interest to people. Availability of resources should also be ensured.
2. Information about the practice should be collected from authentic sources.
3. All the important points should be written.
4. Materials, equipment and aids should be kept in working order.
5. Demonstration should be rehearsed before hand in order to master difficult steps and gain confidence.
6. Advance information regarding time and venue should be circulated and confirmed.

Conducting Demonstration

1. It is essential to make the topic interesting and relevant for the audience.
2. Gather people at site. Make them sit comfortably within visible range so that they can watch demonstrations without difficulty. Introduce people and topic.
3. All materials should be arranged at the site and kept in order to avoid last minute confusion. Give sufficient time to each step. Tell audience clearly about the step being followed and its details. Maintain continuity and flow of speech. There should be harmony between speech and act of demonstration.
4. Keep action simple and neat. Use audio-visual aids to highlight points.

5. Repeat difficult steps.
6. Invite questions and answer them.
7. Invite members of audience to try their hands at demonstration.
8. Let the audience explain what they have learnt.
9. Summarise important points.
10. Provide printed materials, if available, for reference.

Result Demonstration

Result demonstration, as the name indicates, refers to showing net worth of a practice/product like new variety, chemical control of pests, etc. It may be for a single recommended practice or a series of practices that come in sequence with respect to a problem. Result demonstrations do not only establish the value of a practice, but also prove the feasibility of the practice under local conditions.

Planning

1. Demonstration should be planned around definite needs. It requires initial discussion with people to know their resources, problems, interests, etc. The result demonstration should be capable of providing solution to some evident needs. All the people concerned with demonstration like local leaders, farmers, input agencies and specialists should be involved in planning.
2. Selection of demonstration farmers should be done carefully to ensure the following qualities.
   — He should be a dependable person with good background of involvement with extension programmes.
   — He should be a well liked and responsible person with considerable influence in the community.
   — The demonstrator farmer should have land located where many many people will see.
   — The conditions of demonstrator farmer should be representative of average farms of the locality.
   — He should be ready to co-operate in all the required activities and keep records.
   — It provides teaching materials for further use of extension workers.
   — It increases confidence of farmers in new technology.

Limitations

— It is costly.

— It is time taking.
— It is difficult to get good demonstration.
— Much depends on weather and other external factors.

Extension Talk

Speech or talk by extension worker to a small or large group of audience is quite common method to share information. Formal presentation to provide information or technical skills require planning.

Planning

1. Decide purpose of the talk clearly identifying what is to be achieved as outcome. Is it just to create awareness or motivation for action or learning new way of doing.
2. Collect materials on the topic and organise key points.
3. Divide the talk into three parts viz. introduction, body and conclusion as given below :

Introduction

It is essential to plan a motivational approach in the beginning to attract the audience towards the theme of the talk. The speaker should have some understanding about local culture and social environment in order to create emotional appeal. With some experience, one can find out what approach of introduction would be right viz. putting questions to audience, relating economic importance or explaining personal experience. Introduction should not consume more than ten per cent of total time. Purpose of the talk should be spelt out clearly at the end of introduction. Prepare people mentally to expect the sequence of your talk and pay attention to them.

Body of the Talk

Subject matter should be divided into three-four major parts according to availability of time. Each part should be divided into sub-parts. At least seventy-five per cent of time should be devoted to body of the talk. The body should be organized in logical order. Listeners can understand well organised talk easily. Thus many approaches of organisation of talks are possible as below.

Chronological —Arranging talk in order of time like in history, pre-independence and post-independence creates good impression.

Cause-effect — Arrranging materials in this order shows the factors affecting a phenomenon.

Problem-solution — It is better to raise problems and explain solutions one by one.

Compare-contrast — Showing two sides of the phenomenon impresses people instantly.

Each major point should be supported by examples, data or logic. At the end of major point, speaker must summarise the essence and explain the relevance of the point with rest of the talk. Give advance information about each point. Use audio-visual aids at important steps of the talk to provide support to the talk. It is good to repeat key points from time to time.

Summarisation

Summarise by telling the audience in short form what you have covered. Use, suggestive statements to inspire them for action. This part of the talk aims to achieve four-fold goals viz. indicate the end of the talk, summarise the major points and reinforce the central idea. This should not take more than 10-15% of total time.

Important Guidelines for Presentation

1. Appear calm and collected exuberating confidence and enthusiasm.
2. Stand erect. Do not lean over the lectern or platform. Unnecessary movement of any part of your body will distract audience.
3. Maintain eye-contact. People tend to go away mentally if you read the text. Avoid reading from text.
4. Voice must be loud enough to be heard. It is helpful to maintain flexibility.
5. One should choose words carefully according to level of audience. Bookish language should be avoided. Flow of language enhances interest but pace should be adjusted.
6. Watch reaction of audience. Check if voice is audible and visual aids are visible to the audience at the back. Keep question-answer session at the end to clarify doubts. One can plan to interact with audience in the middle of the talk or at important steps.

Checklist for Good Extension Talk

— Speaker has aroused interest of audience in the topic.
— He has stated purpose clearly in 1, 2, 3 and .... terms.
— He moves in organised way
— He explains abstract ideas through examples and arguments
— He uses understandable language

— He uses internal summary every time a major point is made.
— He gives overview, states the point supporting it and reviews them in the end.
— He signals transition from one point to another.
— He uses gestures.
— He adapts pace of delivery
— He changes volume of speech rhythmically
— He exuberates confidence and enthusiasm
— He uses summary to wind up the talk

Meeting

The primary purpose of a meeting is to transact business of an organisation. Meetings are held for a variety of purposes such as sharing information, solving problems, decision making or strategy planning.

Planning for Village Meetings

Even though meeting is a common method, farmers do not often open up before outsiders or in groups. Thus, organisation of meeting requires relaxed atmosphere to stimulate the silent ones to speak. Some points to remember while planning meeting, as given below, need attention.

Venue

The place of meeting should be convenient to each member. It requires quite uninterrupted place to conduct meeting. Farmers should not have any hesitation to assemble at the appointed site. Experiences indicate that farmers have many social considerations regarding visiting each other's places. It is better to keep common place.

Physical Environment

Seating arrangement should be made to facilitate direct interaction. Circular seating arrangement allows members to face each other. Lighting ventilation and source of water should be ensured before hand.

Agenda

It is helpful to announce agenda or meeting early enough so that everyone comes ready with relevant information.

Conditions for Interactive Meeting

Arrangement of physical environment is not enough. In order to stimulate enthusiasm and facilitate participative atmosphere, ground rules should be framed. Above all, the atmosphere of meeting should be friendly. Each one should have equal opportunity to talk and ask question. Negative criticism and rudeness should not be allowed. The following points should be observed :

— Introduction of every group member should be done in the beginning.
— Clear and audible voice is a must
— Good introduction of day's agenda should be made.
— Each member should be helped to contribute
— Remind the dominating member to let others express their points
— Encourage silent or hesitating member to contribute
— Summarise the decisions from time to time to get consensus and let everybody know the progress
— Encourage expression of various viewpoints. Ask people to be specific.
— Call attention to strong disagreement and request for pertinent information
— Keep discussion on track whenever it goes out of context. Remind members of the agenda.
— Listen carefully for hesitations and agreements within the group and bring them out.
— Take preventive steps to check distracting members, tension within group, dominating members, silent members, and low morale.

Techniques to make Meetings lively

It is important to note that members feel interested if the goal of meeting is clear and relevant. They feel attached with the purpose and believe they can do something about it. In order to create sense of belonging and involvement on the part of every member, the leader must use some techniques.

Excitement sharing : In order to create positive atmosphere and put people more in touch with each other, share good news people may have since the last meeting.

Group Achievement : Review each agenda and announce the decisions. At the end, make everyone feel having achieved the task.

Appreciation : Group members should be recognised every time they bring good points in discussion or help resolve the problem.

Group Songs : Songs, especially emotional group songs that indicate value of working together for a cause may be adopted or written for the specific purpose of the group. They grab attention away from thinking, arguing and problem solving.

Brainstorming : In order to get out as many ideas as possible in a limited amount of time, a question may be raised. Everyone has to contribute idea freely. No one should criticise or discuss the ideas in details at the first instance. List of all such free ideas should be put on flip charts or chalk board. At later stage, ideas should be screened, refined and categorised. The group can prioritise or decide ideas as per need.

Role of the Leader/Facilitator in Meeting

The person conducting/facilitating the meeting is known by different names like chair-person, leader or facilitator. Of them, facilitator sounds more democratic indicating co-equal status. Whatever be the name, a facilitator is like a conductor of orchestra. He moderates the contributions of various participants. He helps the members to accomplish decisions in a meeting. Thus, he has the responsibility to remind the group of its task, encourage ideas, test for consensus and help them run the business smoothly. A good facilitator never imposes his ideas rather makes participants feel that they are in charge. He takes the responsibility to articulate group's views and facilitate communication process. In performing his responsibility the leader remains neutral personally. He is alert and sensitive to what each member says. He maintains order and decorum in the group.

Group Discussion

It is a form of discourse or dialogue between two or more people to exchange information of a common topic with an aim to understand and/ or solve the problem.

Group discussion is a very significant method for extension work. It assumes that the members involved in discussion are equal in status and every participant has some experience or information to contribute. It is specially suited to work with adults who prefer sharing of information than being instructed. The members are free to question each other. Thus, group discussion is specially helpful for exchange of experience and information, gaining better understanding of a problem, finding solution to a problem felt by the group, training people in leadership skills and planning a programme of action.

Planning

— Make arrangements for physical facilities viz. sitting place, furniture, public address system, drinking water, etc.
— Inform everyone about time and place.
— Circulate materials needed for discussion
— Arrange for someone to present the issue for discussion alongwith requisite background.
— Keep minimum visual aids like slip chart or chalk board for presenting important points.
— As farmers do not easily open up before experts, it is necessary to plan use of techniques to help every member to share his point and feel a sense of belonging to the group.

Conducting

— Make group comfortable by exchanging greetings and general conversation.
— Seat the group in circle so that each one can see others.
— Motivate silent ones to come up.
— Discourage those who try to monopolise discussions.
— Clarify doubts or vague statements.
— Summarise group's views from time to time.
— Recognise and interpret different point of views present in the group.
— Analyse facts provided by the members
— Encourage critical thinking among members by challenging the assumption and seeking evidences.
— Motivate members to take leading role one by one.

Role of Chairman

— Introduce members
— Announce the topic and purpose of discussion
— Listen to the contributions made by each member carefully.
— Build conducive climate to motivate members to speak freely
— Keep discussion moving on track.
— Promote evaluation of all generalizations
— Protect view points of minority
— Get balanced participation

— Promote group cohesion
— Give summary

Role of Members

Members should talk one at a time and contribute only one point at a time. They should listen attentively and stay on the subject. Members may ask critical questions whenever essential. They should try to promote group harmony.

Role of Experts

In situations when the group does not have requisite technical information, experts may be called in. He should not suggest his own solution rather help the group understand the problem in their location and visualise possible solutions.

Advantages

— It is democratic method giving equal opportunity to each participant.
— It creates high degree of interest.
— It helps people gain skills to work in teams.
— It develops group morale
— It enhances knowledge and critical thinking.

Limitations

— Villages may have factions and hence it may be difficult to organise group-discussion.
— It is difficult to conduct discussion on new topics.
— It is hard to get group consensus
— People are not accustomed to working in group under some discipline.

Exhibition

Exhibition is systematic display of information with the help of variety of methods and media of communication in order to create interests and desire among visitors to adopt. Exhibition is arranged for a variety of purposes as given below.

— Exhibition is arranged to create public interest in new technologies.
— It helps to create goodwill and gain publicity.
— It draws large crowd if coincided with local festival and/or fairs.

— Use of local materials and involvement of farmers will create enthusiasm.
— It influences people to new practices.

Planning

— Determine specific purpose for which exhibition may be organised such as making people aware about practices recommended for profitable orchards or better dairy or to promote good will and publicity for the extension organisation.
— Select a small committee to decide on various aspects of exhibition, at least one to two months in advance.
— Develop written plan of site and arrangement for display
— Decide on schedule of exhibition, materials needed, people to be responsible, etc.
— Exhibits should be labelled legibly and briefly.
— Guides and interpretors should be promptly available with ready information for accurate explanation.
— Relevant literature should be available for distribution
— Models and action exhibits like moving tractor, functional pumping set or bio-gas can be a source of attraction.
— Plan elaborately for public conveniences, fire-fighting equipments, first aid, watch and ward, parking space, garbage spots, etc. so that large crowds can move in and out smoothly.
— Locate and arrange materials for display.
— Involve local people and agencies in organising exhibition.
— There should be visitors attendance book to get comments of the visitors.

Conducting Exhibition

— Maintain sequence and continuity in display of materials.
— Give sufficient attention to layout of space and decoration to give visual appeal. Many national level exhibitions use local symbols and visuals to give attractive orverall impressions. Logos of the extension organisation or indigenous art form can be given prominence.
— Effectiveness of exhibition can be measured by analysing attendance, enquiries and suggestions. Schedules can be developed to get visitors', reactions and sugestions.

Advantages

— It has good publicity value.

— It promotes creative abilities among participants.
— It can also create market for a new product.
— It can fit well with local festive occasion and provide information with entertainment.

Limitations

— It requires lot of time and money, besides investments in preparations.
— It usually turns out to be of good recreation value only.

Field Trip

A field trip is organised excursion for a group of people for the sake of first hand observation of a problem or practice(s) in natural setting. Field trips are organised for a number of objectives as given below:

— It stimulates interest, conviction and action in respect of a specific practice.
— It helps to recognise problems, develop interests and promote adoption.
— It demonstrates feasibility of related practices to the learners in an informal way.

Planning

— Planning for a field trip starts with decision about choice of a particular place for visit. In order to involve people in the educational activity, a committee can be formed consisting of members from participants and officials sponsoring the trip.
— Decide exactly what the trip is supposed to achieve so that details can be planned.
— Decide the places (sites) and practices to be visited.
— Plan for people to explain relevant details and values. Information to concerned people and their readiness can be ensured through advance planning.
— Work out time schedule, routes of visit and people to be introduced.
— Arrange for transport and necessary permission from authorities to make the trip.
— It is better to send extension staff to the site in advance to make local arrangements for visits, stay and board (if needed).
— Participants should be given precise instruction about where and when to meet. Assign responsibilities to participants.

Conducting the Trip

— Emphasize on the purpose of the trip so that it is not taken as a leisure-pleasure activity.
— Provide information on the sites and topics of visit.
— Ask participants to assemble in a manner that everyone can hear, see and discuss conveniently without any obstruction.
— Help them to make notes of important information
— Allow time for questions and answers.
— Adhere to schedule all the time.
— Take preventive action to avoid untoward incidents
— Keep record of attendance and activities. Get photographs for writing news or features.

Follow-up

— Thank the committee, hosts and other concerned people for cooperation.
— Organise follow-up meetings to generate idea for action.
— Write for newspapers or farm magazines to give publicity to the trip.

Extension Campaign

Campaign is concentrated use of different communication methods and media around a theme for a period of time. It is well organised and intensive activity. A campaign creates wide public awareness and provides specific message. Dramatic use of different channels ensures attention and interest. It lasts in the memory of the people and stimulate action.

Examples : Rat control campaign or village cleanliness drive.

Campaigns are well suited to create mass awareness and interest of public about an important theme. It creates conducive environment for adoption.

Planning

— The problem of the campaign should be decided on the basis of local needs. It requires consultations with both leaders and specialists to plan for campaigns.
— Once theme is decided, meeting should be held in villages to fix events, choose dates, arrange for supplies and seek co-operation of all concerned.
— Draw concrete plan highlighting number of activities, dates, sites, materials required (including funds) and persons responsible for activities.

— Choice of methods and media of communication depends on the objective and size of audience to be covered.
— Decide how to involve people in events. Draw list of different people to be informed.
— Select a period suitable to the community, announce the dates well in advance and build enthusiasm of people.

Conducting

— The campaign should begin with something dramatic and interesting. A mass gathering with prominent person creates different image. Such events attract attention of media people as well. Thus, there is widespread publicity and reminder to people through different sources. However, theme or central message of the campaign should be sharply focussed. The campaign should consist of a variety of approaches like meetings, tours, newspaper articles, leaflets, exhibition etc. as given below.

Meetings

Meetings of different kinds can attract people, like meeting with popular personality, scientists, meeting in the village or meeting with leaders on relevant theme. The meetings may be organised at public places alongwith one or two more events viz. screening films or contests.

Tours

Tours can show results to people who have never tried. Working of an effective club or good cultivation of new crop may be shown through tours. They create interest and add to publicity value.

Newspaper articles

Feature articles, reports of events and advertisements in local newspapers can help in reinforcing messages.

Leaflets, Posters and Wall Newspapers

Leaflets may provide information whereas posters remind people of the important messages through slogans, or attractive visuals. Wall newspapers can be initiated in village communities to provide regular information in local dialect.

Exhibition

Villagers have habit of attending *melas* or exhibitions. Scientific exhibitions provide good opportunity to attract gatherings.

Social Service

Contribution of day's labour by the people for a common cause like plantation of trees, cleaning garbages, building community house, etc. create goodwill and public support.

Contests

Organising contest among people for best co-operation, best home or healthy children, good orchard, cattle, etc. can generate sense of competition and accomplishment. Such events can give opportunity to organise scientific panels, or lectures.

A combination of above methods can be chosen and campaign may be run for a week or fortnight with sequence of activities. It should culminate in a grand closing ceremony with reports on different events, prize distribution and reinforcement of messages.

Evaluation

Evaluation is essential to know the achievement. Plan systematic evaluation to help in collecting evidence during the programme and afterwards. Interview people, leaders and collect observations on changes as well as reactions. Evaluation should finally help in planning improvement and record changes made by people as a result of campaign.

Advantages

- A large number of farmers can be covered quickly.
- It creates conducive environment to popularise other methods.
- It gives quick result at lower costs.
- It builds trust of people.
- This is quite effective in situation where whole community needs to be encouraged to adopt a practice.

Limitations

- It requires thorough preparation and intensive work.
- It is applicable to limited themes.
- It requires co-operation of people from various organisations, which is often hard to get.

Field Day

Field day is an organised gathering of farmers, extension workers and experts at the site of result demonstration for sharing information and experience about the practice.

It is an important extension method to enhance utility of result demonstration. On this day, site of result demonstration is visited by the farmers with the following objectives :

— To learn about feasibility of new practice under local conditions.
— To observe and hear experiences of fellow farmers.

Planning

— Decide the purpose of field day i.e. to show specific stage of crop, result of new practice or a particular operation.
— Select site which is approachable by road and there is sufficient space required for meeting, exhibition, parking, etc.
— Decide time and place.
— Arrange for transport
— Arrange for exhibition and meeting.

Conducting

— Take the farmers to the crop site. Take care that everybody can see and listen to the narrations. Explain the points lucidly.
— Take the farmers round the exhibition hall, if any.
— Start technical session with scientists. Let scientists explain the technology. Invite questions and clarifications.
— Distribute literature.
— Serve refreshment.

Advantages

— It further helps to popularise the result of demonstration.
— It has good publicity value

Limitations

— If the growth of crop is poor or field day is poorly organised, farmers get wrong impression.
— It is difficult to gather genuine farmers.

Radio

Radio is most popular mass media, among majority of rural people. Transistor radio sets are cheap and convenient to use. There is no problem of electricity maintenance and repair.

Special Features of Radio

— It is cheap.
— It is portable.
— It provides information entertainment and education.
— It can quickly transmit messages in most remote areas.
— Distance learning is possible through radio.
— It is helpful in forming public opinion.
— Listener can get the message even while engaged in other activities.

Limitations

— Radio alone cannot bring change.
— Listeners have no control over content or speed of message.
— It is difficult to transmit complicated messages through radio.

Modes of Programme Presentation

Radio programmes are presented in the form of news, interviews, discussion, documentaries, drama, quiz, question-answer etc.

News covers many different topics in short time. Interesting facts and stories of current human interest are broadcast at regular intervals.

Documentaries

— Documentaries are special programmes on events of past, present or future interests. They are different from news in the sense that topic of current or historical importance are treated in depth. It is collection of a variety of materials with narratives.

Interviews : Interviews of prominent personalities and members of the audience create interest. Sometimes experts and other persons involved in an important action may also be interviewed to cater to the interest of the audience.

Discussion : This format uses a number of people giving views on a topic. The participants may be experts or just people having information on topic of concern. Panel discussions require a moderator to co-ordinate discussion and bring consensus.

Magazine : Magazine programmes can combine a number of formats like news, interviews, drama and a number of topics can be covered.

Dramatic : Dramatic programmes include such serials or fictional works which tell complete story in one or more instalments. There may be one or more character and story should be developed through dialogue of characters.

*Spot Announcements :*These are brief comments (10-60 seconds) between, musical numbers or programmes. They provide important information or suggestion for action. These are basically advertisements of some development idea/message.

Quiz and Questions-answers : Quiz and question-answer programmes are good ways to involve audience and assess knowledge with interest. Audience may be asked to send questions or problems, which may be answered by presenter or prominent personality in interesting manner.

Rural Broadcasts

In India, radio broadcasting started as far back as 1927. All India Radio started specialised unit called Farm and Home unit in 1966 to cater to the rural audience. Rural programmes are broadcast by all stations in local dialects. The programmes include hard core technical recommendations, field-based programmes covering festivals, meetings, functions, etc. and interview, recording of folk music, folk songs, agricultural quiz, spot announcements and documentaries. Many different types of programmes have been tried successfully for providing information in interesting manner like Farm School or Air and Mike in the village.

Farm School on Air

Farm School on Air was broadcast from many stations having farm and home units. This was a novel programme in collaboration with State Department of Agriculture and State Agriculture University. All India Radio developed strategy to deliver farm information systematically to farmers in far flung rural areas. Literate farmers with access to radio and evidence of interest and influence in agriculture were selected with the help of the State Department of Agriculture. These farmers were supposed to serve as opinion leader for disseminating scientific information to average farmers. Programmes were divided into lessons. Experts were selected to present the programmes in slow pace by repeating the key points at the end of each programme questions were broadcasts. The listeners were encouraged to send their doubts and questions. Tests were also conducted and registered farmers received certificates.

Field-based Programmes

Studies have indicated that farmers like to hear progressive farmers and known experts. Local fairs, festivals and events attract them. Folk music and songs add local flavour. Programmes recorded outside are preferred than those produced in studio. It is generally suggested to keep 70% field based programmes and only 30% studio based programmes. Agricultural information need to be synchronised with the activities being taken up in the field. Rural broadcasters must have empathy for the woes of the listeners in order to locate appropriate sites, festivals, talents, etc. which can add local flavour and make programmes interesting. Rural broadcasts can be energised by creative use of folk songs and stories to convey developmental messages.

Radio Drama

It has been found that dramatic presentation of even technical information attract farmers. Dramatic presentation of technical programmes has been tried successfully in Nepal. The programme 'Budi Ama and JTA' featuring two characters old lady and JTA (grassroot extension worker) provided information on farm problems in interesting manner. In each episode the old lady began with her farm and home problem and the extension worker in a bid to ease out her problem, narrated the solution. This was liked by farmers and the programme ran for several years.

Programmes with Local Bias

Farm broadcasts must have precise and locally relevant message. Radio programmes should be synchronised with the timings of agricultural operations and programmes of agricultural development being implemented by the state. This will link farmers with ongoing development efforts. It has been reported that Radio DZLB situated in the University of Philippines at Las Banos aired programmes with information about certain seed developed by International Rice Research Institute (IRRI) in the morning and farmers started enquiring about the supply by the afternoon. Thus, need-based situation-specific broadcast have appealed.

Use of Radio in Extension Work

How can radio be used in extension work apart from encouraging individual listening? One way tried in India and many other countries is called Rural Radio Forum (*Churcha Mandal*).

Rural Radio Forum is local discussion group organised by development worker. Community listening and discussion are encouraged with the help of extension worker. Community radio sets are provided for group listening. Advance information is provided about programmes to be broadcast and the group discusses the programme. Farmers reaction on relevance of the topic, difficulties in listening, queries, etc. are recorded by the extension workers. Such feedback are sent to the radio station for modifications in programmes. Thus, the lacuna of the programmes are fed back to the radio station. Extension workers may also record useful programmes of current importance on audio tape. This can be supported by extension literature of local relevance. Audio tapes can be played with the village groups at convenient time and discussions can be organised.

Local Radio/Community Radio

Looking to the popularity of radio as medium of communication and its effectiveness in development, All India Radio (AIR) ventured into a new phase of broadcasting by experimenting with the concept of local radio station. A local radio station serves a small area (a district or so) with similar agro-climatic and cultural situations. The programmes are supposed to reflect local culture and aspirations. They are supposed to support on-going developmental programmes. Field-based programmes using local talents, give voice to people's views. Local culture finds more air time. Community service programmes should provide opportunity to people, their organisation and development organisations to broadcast matters of information. Radio thus becomes voice of the people and catalyst in development. Unlike regular radio, extension workers can find air time.

Audio-Cassette Technology (ACT)

Tape recorder or audio-cassette tape is now very common medium in Indian homes for listening to music. The technology has become cheaper and accessible. Experiences in many developing nations suggest new possibilities for use in extension work.

Special Features of ACT

— It is easy to operate.
— Message of local relevance can be recorded and played.
— Audience may stop, rewind and listen at convenience.
— Local music, songs and people's opinion, talks can also be recorded.
— Battery operated portable sets are also available.

ACT gives audience the choice regarding content of message. Technical messages can be designed systematically keeping the characteristics of audience in mind. Pre-recorded talks of technical experts may compensate for lack of expertise of grassroot extension workers.

How to use ACT in Extension Work?

— The special features of ACT make them most amenable for application in extension situation for passing information or conducting group discussion. ACT can be used both for individual and group listening. Individual listening is possible if the farmers own ACT or it is made available through extension agency. Besides, tape with standardised messages can be multiplied and distributed to those owning ACT sets.
— Tapes can have recorded technical talks of technical experts on topics relevant to audience needs. Local flavour can be given to the content by recording local music, songs and references of known farmers. Local talents like progressive farmers, influential individuals and singers can be recorded to enhance element of interest in the programme. Tapes can use a variety of interesting formats like conversation, drama, question and answer, interview, etc. Slow pace, quick review of materials covered and short suggestive summaries can increase the effectiveness of communication.

Various Applications of ACT

Colle (1975) described four different applications of audio-cassette technology as group listening device, aid to field worker, supplementary device for training and at-home information delivery system for rural dwellers.

Listening Device : The listening group gathers at convenience or pre-scheduled time unlike radio where the time of broadcast is fixed. Further, the tape can be stopped or replayed at the request of listeners thereby giving control in the hands of audience. Group may also record their questions, experiences or message on blank side of a cassette.

Tool/Aid for Field Worker : The field worker may take pre-recorded messages to the audiences and play as per need. The range of message to be provided is not limited by field workers' limited knowledge. Standardised messages in format of interest to the audience can be presented. Thus, authentic information on subjects of choice can supplement person-to-person communication.

Training Tool : Audio-cassette can be used to train field-level workers (para professionals) in scarce skills with pre-recorded messages.

At Home Information Delivery : Another way to use audio-cassette technology is to provide audience with the tape and machine at home so that they can listen when, where and as frequently they wish. Field workers can place the machine in households and return later to answer question or receive request. Thus, field worker can become master of learning resources on a range of subjects.

The experiences with audio-cassette technology in developing nations suggest that there is need to identify modes of presentations with appeal to rural audience. There is good scope to use indigenous materials like local language conversational style, folk music, etc. to stimulate ruralites. Now that audio-cassette machines are readily available, audio-tapes can be prepared to meet local information needs.

Television

Television has unique advantages over other mass media. While it provides sound, vision and movement. It can reach largest number of people in shortest possible time. It is a medium unlike any other. TV screen is small and depends on close-ups. People can watch sitting in their homes. Television viewing does not demand extra strains to go out or read a book and the message are pre-selected, sorted out to present in simple manner. The medium is quite suitable for subjects that require dramatized presentation, identification of objects, live demonstration of complex technical process depicting animated presentation and presentation of experiences, places, processes unfamiliar to viewers.

What Television can or cannot do

As a mass medium TV leads to awareness, contributes to information and helps to form opinion. Before the farmers are motivated to action, televised information may create awareness and interest. However, local demonstration and interpersonal communication are required to convince them. TV is good in exposing people to a whole range of new ideas and experiences. Programme on agriculture have immediate effect if ideas are put forward at a time when they need them most, deal with subject about which farmers do not have pre-fixed notion. If programmes are supportive to efforts made by extension or advisory services working in the locality, the changes are more likely to come.

Limitations

It is centralized mass medium i.e. programmes are produced in distant urban environment and so may not be appropriate for all viewers alike. Those who cannot afford costly inputs recommended by TV cannot benefit. Language of TV is quite sophisticated for rural viewers.

Agricultural Programmes on TV

The farmers like others view television to spend leisure time in agreeable manner. Thus, we must provide entertainment alongwith messages for improvement of the farm and home. The factors involved in television programmes for the farmers are timing when should agriculture programme be telecast, frequency, length of the programme and mode of presentation. Whatever, be the content of the programme, good quality is expected not only in visual but also in audio terms. In producing agricultural programmes, both studio and outdoor broadcasting (OBs) have a place since outdoor recordings bring a sense of immediacy and understanding to the viewers. Demonstration on farming methods brought to farmers by television have great value of making converts to better farm practices. Farmers respond readily to what is said by other farmers. Realistic scenes of local people in native dialect attract attention of farmers. Agricultural programmes must be factual. Use of still films and balance between studio and field based production is a must.

Growth of Television in India

Television programmes started in India on September 15, 1959 on experimental basis for a 40 kms area around New Delhi. First school television was started in October 1961 for schools of Delhi. In 1965, the general service programmes were introduced for one hour on four days a week. It became a daily service by August 15, 1965. A special programme for farmers called 'Krishi Darshan' was launched on January 26, 1967.

The rural programmes are now telecast from all centres and low power transmitters to familiarise rural viewers with latest technical knowledge about farming, weather forecasts, etc. as much as about personal health, hygiene, education and family welfare. Country's second television came up on October 2, 1972 followed by Srinagar, Amritsar, Calcutta, Madras and Lucknow. From August 1, 1975 Doordarshan had undertaken the satellite Instructional Television Experiment(SITE) one of the most ambitious projects in the field of mass communication. it was a one year project covering 2,400 villages spread over in six states. SITE aimed to improve rural primary school education, provide teachers training, improve agriculture, health and hygiene and nutritional practices and contribute to family planning and national integration. Community TV sets had been established in the villages for viewing. SITE's agricultural programmes disseminated information on dryland farming advice on poultry and animal husbandry, recommendation of practices for crops, etc. The end of SITE was followed by SITE continuity projects providing installation of six terrestrial transmitters. Another significant event that determined rapid expansion of TV services was the coverage of the Asiad games in November, 1982. In 1982, India introduced its own multipurpose satellite called INSAT-1A which was used for telecasting, telecommunication, meteorology and radio. It was on August 15, 1982 that national programmes were relayed simultaneously from all centres. INSAT-IB led to a major expansion of television broadcasting in India and television broadcasting took a new form. The rapid expansion of transmission facilities also led to establishment of new production centres. Thus, TV which started in 1959 on experimental basis has spread through length and breadth of the country.

Television expansion in India has always been rationalised on the plea that TV can revolutionise rural areas by providing information and education. However, this is a common knowledge that due to predominance of sponsored programmes and interest of commercial organisations, TV has become predominantly a medium of cheap entertainment for middle class educated Indians. TV has shown little enthusiasm and activity to serve the needs of the poor ruralites. Agricultural programmes are most of the times dull and dry. Some of the criticisms labelled against rural television programmes are as below :

— Inspite of the access, all the rural people, specially poor cannot afford to buy television sets.

— There is little enthusiasm among urban producers to make programmes interesting for the large majority of ruralites. As a result, rural programmes have very low viewership.
— The themes shown on the television have little relevance to the problems and development efforts going on in the area.
— There is strong emphasis on entertainment based programmes and commercials. Television programmes promote consumerism than development.
— Handful of community sets provided in some states remained defunct due to lack of electricity, proper maintenance or democratic management.

Use of Television in Extension Work

A Rural Television (RTV) project was launched by the FAO in 1974 in Sudan. The aim of the project was to disseminate specifically designed programmes for the tenant farmers. TV was introduced to inform, instruct and motivate. Generators were also provided alongwith TV sets to each village. Existing village clubs which served as a forum for social gathering were used to form TV viewing club. Each selected village was asked to nominate one person as TV club monitor to take care of TV set, generator and form TV viewing club to initiate discussion on rural programmes. He would also initiate activities for adoption of ideas shown in TV programmes. The monitors were trained to perform these tasks. Though the programme continued, there were few problems in effective functioning like monitors were not always active and discussions were less frequent. Later, efforts were taken to keep close contact with TV monitors and use TV programmes and village discussion in field extension programmes as well. While it is generally believed that TV can be used successfully as a means of communication to rural areas, Sudan Rural Television Project showed that rural TV can be effective if complemented by inter-personal communication.

Video

Video is an important aspect of advancement in communication technology. It provides the facility of audio-visual communication like film or television but with less complexity and added advantages. This is the reason why video has spread all over the world with electrifying speed. It is now easily accessible in India. Government of India with the support of the World Bank has special plans to use video in agricultural extension work. Miniaturisation of video equipment and easy availability in cities and villages alike make this small medium appropriate for extension work.

Video is unique medium for audio-visual communication. It is decentralized and thus useful to communicate local messages among groups with similar characteristics. The images are sharp unlike films. Videos have smaller viewing screen with its fixed height to width ratio of 3 : 4. It is a medium greatly dependent on close-ups unlike films, which have greater resolution (more picture elements per frame). Unlike television, video does not require large broadcasting equipments or infrastructure. Small screen of video, placed in quiet corner of home, provides many plus points. Audiences, relaxed in bed or seats, with eyes fixed on the small screens are more concentrated.

Advantages of Video

— It has high quality audio-visual recording system to portray reality within limited time and resource.
— Instant playback facilities for pause and replay at any time allows viewers to review materials at will.
— Audience can exercise control over content and time of viewing.
— It is available in very light weight, battery-operated and highly portable form.
— Ease in operation provides ready access to almost any one. Video equipments do not require sophisticated training to operate.
— Local problems, scenes, real life situations, etc. can be shared to stimulate empathy and discussion.
— Many unusual scenes, off season crops or cultivation, distant objects and minute operations can be easily projected.
— Video can provide immediate feedback to learners on their performance as they display certain skills.
— It is very effective in creating attitudes and emotions by use of various techniques and effects.

Disadvantages

— Video script writing is difficult and time taking.
— Video quality when transferred from one tape to another, gets degenerated.
— Local availability of video-equipment, repairing services, spare parts etc. is essential to ensure smooth running.

— Trained talents in production are not readily available.

Production of Training Video

Video lessons to become integral part of training must match with the objectives of training as much as with the background of learners. Eventhough precise norms for producing instruction video for ruralites have not been spelt out, the socio-cultural and personal background of farmers demand attention in designing such programmes. There is definite importance of language, pace of programme, visual appearance, etc. in designing video for instruction.

Thus, it requires initial field investigation and consultations with the farmers to determine content and its treatment. The existing level of attitude, knowledge skills and beliefs need to be studied. The popular appeals, visual perception, interests etc. can be known through audience analysis. Thus, video programme production requires step-by-step work as below.

— Identification of target audience, their educational and socio-cultural context.
— Definition of production objective, choice of content and format.
— Script writing and recording.
— Production of final version.

Characteristics of Instructional Programmes for Ruralites

— One thing for sure, instructional programme should be of short duration like 10-20 minutes in order to make due consideration for capability of human absorption, attention span, etc. If long duration programmes are inevitable, they may be broken into parts.
— The programme should be simple and non-ostentatious. Unlike commercial programmes, costly sets, customers, etc. are not the prime concern. In fact, undesirable distractions in terms of scenes should be avoided. Clear specification of message in systematic manner is needed.
— It should be audible and clearly visible. Realistics scenes of local people in local dialect create interest among farmers.
— The purpose of the programme should be spelt out within first-two minutes of introduction. A catchy dramatic opening helps in gaining attention of audience. Repetition of major points and an appeal for motivation are needed for closure.

Various Applications of Video

Video as an instructional medium can be most appropriate if recognition or discrimination of relevant motion stimuli is required. It can teach rules, procedures and skills. It is useful to orient learners to places, objects, strange behaviours, etc. Moreover, video can be used conveniently with or without guide. Print support and can be followed by actual work to help model new behaviours. There are many opportunities in extension training where video can be conveniently used as described below :

Orientation : Audience (farmers) can be introduced about to such things as the campus, the institution, the course details etc. by showing clippings.

Feedback : During the skills practice sessions, the videotaped materials can be shown, critiqued and kept for comparison.

Documentation : Many a time it is hard to recall the events of a training session for records, reporting or public relation purposes. The activities thus documented can act as resource for prospective training.

Evaluation of Performance : Video can very well be used to illustrate the trainers' behaviour, trainees' performance, training processes, physical facilities etc. and provide a wealth of management data to help evaluate performance of training courses.

Training Video—Some Considerations : There can be two types of videotapes for use during training i.e. readymade commercial or specifically produced for the course. Videotapes can be purchased in case they are available commercially. Such commercially produced video must meet the objectives of the course. It is also essential to evaluate their suitability for the levels of participants in terms of language, appropriateness of message, technical quality, etc. The length of the programme must not be more than 30 minutes, in any case. The quality of presentation and authenticity must be checked thoroughly before use during training.

One may, however, think of producing video in case such materials are of perennial importance and can be repeatedly used in many training situations of significance. Training video need not meet the standard of entertainment video in terms of expensive sets, decorations or artwork, sophisticated presentation styles or so on the other hand simple, field based, short and localised productions enhance effectiveness of training.

Before producing an effective video some preliminary investigations about learners characteristic is a must. Training video for farmers requires several considerations in terms of language, pace of commentary, type of visuals, extent of repetition, nature of reinforcements, etc.

How to use Video during Training?

If one reviews the current uses of video in extension training contexts, videos will be found to be easy escapes to pass unstructured time or fill the gap. Often a film with matching title (with the training) may be played in the hope of creating interest but without concrete plans to achieve that. There are four well defined steps to help effective use of video in training, viz. preparation, playback and summarization of learning points.

Preparation for showing : It is necessary to check that the tape is of the correct size and standards for the available equipments. The trainer needs to preview the tape and identify important points of learning. The equipments need to be tried before hand. Arrangement of seats, lighting and the video set (monitor) must be done keeping in view the room and activities to be carried out during or after viewing.

Provide Instruction : The learners need to be told beforehand about what they will see and why it is essential for them. Discussions may be held about what they already know about the topic. Key concepts may be defined, questions can be posed and supplementary media like work book may be introduced for use after viewing.

Play the Videotape : Light, volume of sound and picture should be adjusted for clear viewing and audibility. The attitude of the trainer towards the programme is also important. Lack of attention on the part of the trainer of his frequent movements out of the class may also be taken negatively. After playing the films for planned duration, it may be replayed on the demand of the audience all over again or at certain designated points. The trainer must monitor learners or their reactions during viewing sessions.

Summarise Learning Points : After the film has been viewed, discussion may be initiated. The doubts may be clarified and concepts explained. It is essential to summarize the major points of learning. If possible, notes may be distributed for reference.

Video can be used as training aid in many ways. It may be a self-sufficient medium used alone to provide required skills along with the trainers' interventions or it can be supplemented with manual, workbook or any other type of print support. Video can be used in training to achieve objective only in part or complete.

Use of Video in Extension Work

Video has been used successfully in extension work in India and abroad. Some cases of video have been narrated below :

Taprana Video Project : The project initiated by National Dairy Research Institute, Karnal, Haryana, aimed to use video in order to organise dairy co-operatives in a village inhabited by resource poor farmers. Video tapes of dairy co-operative running in neighbouring villages were shown to stimulate lively discussion among Taprana's inhabitants. Video helped farmers to realize the constraints of low price, role of middle men, quality control etc. Technical know-how was also presented with the help of video tapes. A coummunity worker was used as animator to stimulate discussion among farmers with the help of videos focussed on problems existing in the villages. Locally relevant scene of neighbouring villages having similar problems catalysed imagination of farmers. Thus, video was successfully used in creating dialogue between farmers and community workers.

Saharanpur Experiment : Centre for Development of Instructional Technology (CENDIT), New Delhi carried out an experiment using portable video recorder as medium of communication among villages in Uttar Pradesh. The team found that usual films and documentation on agriculture and family planning were unable to stimulate farmers because they were far removed from the problems being faced. Thus the CENDIT team lived in villages to record thoughts and actions of people and show it to them. Ideas of villages, identifiable scenes and problems catalysed fierce discussion about real problems. The villagers articulated their misery and oppressions. This also helped in deep realizations of the problem and formation of groups to tackle these problems. In fact, at one stage people were given opportunities to handle the equipments themselves. The results were exciting in terms of capturing real scene and through opinions of villagers.

Both these projects and other experiences around the world proved efficacy of video in communicating developmental messages to farmers.

CIRCULAR LETTERS

This is a letter reproduced with same content and information to many people periodically or on some occasions. It is good way to keep regular touch with farmers and to communicate timely information in a personal way. It is a good way to provide information about new technologies to farmers quickly. It is also very helpful to invite farmers on the occasion of field day, demonstration, exhibitions, etc.

Points for writing Circular Letters

— Decide specific theme for writing
— Plan the form, text and illustration.
— It is better to keep the letter to the point and provide only important information.
— Use simple language as far as possible quoting terms popularly known by farmers.
— Highlight key information by underlining or putting bold letters.
— Keep the tone of the letter personal.
— The contents of circular letters are better suited for news, announcements and how-to-do type of information.
— Keep the size of the letter to one page only.
— Use coloured paper.
— Choose suitable illustrations to highlight your message.

Advantages

— It can reach large number of people.
— It can be preserved and used at convenience.
— It is economic.

Limitations

— It is of little use in areas with low literacy.
— It loses significance if not prepared carefully.

RURAL PUBLICATIONS

Printed words carry credibility. Increasing rural literacy has widened the scope of using printed materials for the farmers. Eventhough majority of farmers is illiterate, there is always someone in the immediate environment to read out to them. Thus, potential consumers of extension publications are more than number of literates. There are other advantages of using publication, as below:

Economy

— Per unit cost of production comes out cheaper if number of farmers reached is considered.

Convenience

— One can read at leisure as many times as required.

Access

— It can reach a large number of people quickly.

Compatibility with other Methods and Media

One can use publications alongwith other methods and media to reinforce the message.

RURAL PRESS

Rural press refers to those newspapers and periodicals operating in and for country side covering rural themes and satisfying the tastes of rural readers. Four-fold criteria for identifying rural press, according to Malhan (1977) are as given below.

— Place of publication should be outside metropolitan towns, state capitals or big cities.
— Content of the paper should focus mostly on rural community, their socio-economic and cultural, educational problems, their thinking and aspirations.
— Newspaper should use spoken language or idiom of the rural readers.
— These dailies, periodicals, wall papers and wall sheets should be read mostly by rural readers.

However, Indian Rural Press association has fixed the criteria that 40 per cent of editorial space should be devoted to news and views on agriculture, community development and Panchayat Raj but reporting on agriculture remains a low priority area to the Indian newspapers, with honourable exception. English language press is extremely urban. There is no mechanism at all to encourage original grassroot reporting on agriculture. The bulk of news appearing in national or regional dailies are based on ministers' speeches, press-briefings or pronouncement of the government department, parliament debates, etc. Agriculture reporting rung in the ladder of prestige. Agricultural information covering people's problems, local self-government, agrarian reform, rural organisation and infrastructure, etc. can create awareness about existing situation and guide them to precise place and person for seeking help. It can throw light on instances of injustice. The newspapers covering a small jurisdiction such as a district or town can serve local interests and rural leaders better. Thus, the concept of rural press is one of the friend, philosopher and guide for the readers. It is press of, for and by the rural people in their own languages and themes of interest. No doubt, agricultural information and development messages are critical inputs for the ruralites. A project of development journalism launched by an Indian daily newspaper in English, as given below, proved the value of such information.

PROJECT VILLAGE CHHATERA — A CASE

The project popularly known as Chhatera project focussed its attention on a small village 'Chhatera' situated 25 miles north-west of New Delhi. *The Hindustan Times* started a regular fortnightly column describing life in village Chhatera. 'Our village Chhatera' appeared on the cover story in a Sunday magazine of *The Hindustan Times* and continued for years week after week. A team of enterprising reporters wrote about the village with rare sensitivity and perception, giving detailed story of rural situation. They wrote about village Chaupal, marriage, festivals, day to day activities aspiration, institutions, profession, etc. The problems of erratic power supply, rainfall, village disputes, etc. were reported with good photographs. Even the view points on controversial topics were reported. Every week village problems and matters were treated afresh. Thus, the features attracted attention of a wide variety of readers. Besides it proved as a catalyst in bringing various services and benefits. Solution to village problems were available due to attention of authorities and other concern citizens. The village got a rural bank, new road, a bridge, machines, etc. Above all the faction ridden village community got together (Gupta, 1982).

Agricultural Reporting in Kerala

'Mathrubhoomi' one of leading dailies threw open one page every week for reporting agriculture and allied topics, with the help of scientists of the State Department and Agricultural University. Soon after other newspapers followed the trend. It is usual in Kerala that newspapers publish articles on agriculture once every week. Kerala Agricultural University has taken steps to avail of the opportunities offered by the newspapers. They provide regular features and items of topical interests. The university also provides exclusive materials to newspapers. The university has taken steps to appoint scientists for this purpose. So that steady flow of materials is maintained (National Seminar, 1983).

'Batabaran' — A Wall Newspaper

The Nepal Forum of Environmental Journalist (NFEJ) with assistance from the World Conservation Union (IUCN) has been publishing a wall newspaper, 'Batabaran' (Environment) with the objective of providing news to rural areas and create environmental awareness. The major focus is on simple text, real life stories and lot of pictures and graphics. So that readers and rural areas can understand easily. It caters to the needs of large majority of new-literates and village influentials. Success stories of efforts of conservation and environmental protection are highlighted. Stories are timed with activities in the local areas. The newspaper also publishes issues of national and international events related with environment. The writers of the 'Batabaran', mostly journalist members of NFEJ visit villages to collect true stories and write in people's language. Villager's opinion about content and presentations of the paper are taken regularly by the members of NFEJ. The wall newspapers has been successful in providing villagers with relevant news and support for literacy in Nepal (DCR No. 79, 1992/4).

Function of Rural Press

The number of rural newspapers operating in and for rural areas, covering rural themes is negligible. However, they are good links between development organisations and people. Extension agencies can make good use of them. Rural press can serve many functions. Rural press can serve as medium of continuous education. It can become mouth piece of people by highlighting their culture, problems and aspirations. Progress of development programmes can be reported in investigative manner to make people conscious. It can guide local people about help available with various development agencies. It can ensure dialogue between people and their leaders.

Farm Journals

Farm journals are considered as important tools to disseminate relevant development messages to the rural audience. In past, Bengal Agricultural Gazette under the editorship of Mr. Robert Knight was the first governmental effort to disseminate agricultural information to Indian farmers. Plantation news was started next to cater to the needs of the planters. Mahatma Gandhi, the legendary leader had started *Harijan* to reach the masses. The weekly *Harijan* also dealt with agriculture and cottage industries in simple language. The first farm magazine in Hindi *Krishi Sudhar* was brought out from Agra (1914) followed by *Krishi* (1918). *Zamin Dyot* — a farm weekly was published at Nellore, Andhra Pradesh in 1928. *Agriculture and Livestock* was started by Imperial Council of Agricultural Research by 1930, which was later renamed and published as *Indian Farming*. *Indian Journal of Agricultural Science* was published in 1931. Bihar Government had initiated *Gaon* in 1938. Another venture *Vasundhara* was published by Kolhapur Ryot Sewa Sangh of Maharashtra. Another Hindi farm weekly *Krishak Jagat* was brought out from Nagpur in the same year. In 1947 the Indian Council of Agricultural Research started Hindi Journal *Kheti* followed by *Phal Phool*. The number of farm journals must have touched 400 marks by now. However, all of them do not publish exclusively for the farmers. State Agricultural University, Institute of Indian Council of Agricultural Research (ICAR), Voluntary organisations and input organisations now bring out farm journals. Most of these farm journals have small readership. Successful ventures among them include *Changi Kheti* (Punjabi), *Haryana Kheti* and *Shetkari* (Marathi). Besides, *Sevagram, Krishak Jagat,* and *Kisan Bharati, Intensive Agriculture, Indian Farming* and *Kheti* are quite popular. Inspite of several advantages of farm journals, it is difficult for most of them to mobilise more than a thousand readership. Most of the government sponsored publications are highly subsidised.

Problems with Farm Journals

The farm journals suffer from a number of problems as below :

Financial Problem

Apart from government sponsored journals, the private efforts are beset by sheer struggle for economical survival. Low readership, inability to attract big advertisement in rurally oriented development journal pose economic hurdles to sustain longer.

Delayed Publication

Most of the journals coming out of State Agriclutural Universities run months late. Thus, the contents of the months for which they are meant, become irrelevant.

Lack of Trained Farm Journalists/Editor

Farm journals suffer from genuine problem of finding worthwhile articles written in vernacular language for the farmers. People trained in rural journalism are hard to find.

Technical Jargon

Use of technical jargons is so much so that reading and comprehension is difficult for low-literate or neo-literate readers.

Content and Presentation

Choice of contents is too general. Some types of articles are repeated year after year. There is little involvement feedback or input from the farmers. The articles are mostly oriented towards agricultural technologies. Socio-economic and situational problems of farmers are seldom highlighted. Similarly, presentation is mechanical, straight jacket and dull in most cases.

This is not to say that farm journals in the country are not effective. Rather, they still have to adapt the materials from farmers' point of view. Studies on farm journals have clearly suggested need for revamping content and presentation of farm journals.

Suggestions for Improvement of Farm Journals

1. Farm journals must cater to miscellaneous interests of farmers and provide content to suit resources as well as tastes of different

categories of readers. This requires familiarity with target group, their environment, crops, living, festivals, etc. The contents must reflect these interests. Presentation of articles should also be interesting. Straight-cut details on technologies look too mechanical. Feature articles using direct personal references and local examples may enliven the material. Besides, success stories of farmers, agricultural news, farmers' experiences, discussion on relevant indigenous practices may also be tried.

2. Use of illustrations and photographs should be promoted. Clearly identifiable photographs or even line drawing may add to reading ease of texts. Close-up photographs showing details are particularly desirable.
3. Editor of farm journals should preferably be agricultural graduate trained in farm Journalism/Journalism and exposed to rural life and farming. He should screen articles and take efforts to encourage authors to write originally for the farmers. He should conduct studies to gauge farmers' reactions and preferences. He may formulate clear-cut guidelines for authors for writing. He should screen, modify and adapt articles suitable to readers.
4. There is urgent present need to simplify technical terms and find ways to ease the burden of measurement units. It requires effort to collect local equivalent technical terms and standardize them for consistency in use.
5. Layout, typography, preparation of illustration, colour scheme of printing and proof reading should not be left to chance. Preparation of dummy out of revised proofs may ensure better publications.
6. Accuracy in reporting of technical information is a must. Names of chemicals, varieties and their doses must be carefully checked.

Writing for Rural Readers — Some Tips

Most reading materials meant for normal readers with formal education and exposure to printed media, do not fare well with rural readers. Writing for people deeply rooted in oral culture with very little or no exposure to written words is a challenge. It calls for innovations in written communication. Some of the key-points needing attention are given below :

1. The theme/topic of writing should be intimately related with the life and problems of the readers.

2. The idea to be communicated should be kept as simple as possible. The title should be catchy.
3. The idea should be introduced in the lead part by informing about the contents in advance.
4. Each major point should be covered separately giving suitable sub-titles.
5. The vocabulary should be easy to spell and pronounce. Spoken words with appeal should be preferred.
6. Popular folk tales with known names and characters can create emotional appeal. Sentences should be short, indirect and narrative in form. Average sentence-length of 6 to 8 words is convenient for low literates.
7. The type face should be big and bold.
8. Layout of the page should be soothing to eye by giving enough white space.
9. It is better to support text by giving matching pictures or line drawings, side by side.
10. Use examples and analogies easily understood by the target group.
11. Repeat the key points in the end and even underline them.

A model of publication gaining popularity now-a-days with writers interested in easy to understand text, uses two-page spread. One page includes the text containing an advance organiser to introduce the topic in a sentence, a title indicating the idea, sub-headings, presentation of information in paragraph format. On the right hand of the page, diagrams and explanations are given (Hynka, 1979).

SELF-HELP FARM JOURNALISM — A CASE

All India Arecanut Growers' association in Puttur, Karnataka started publishing farm journal *Akike Pathrika* in Kanada languages. It has several new features, as below :

1. It concentrates on articles written by farmers on the basis of successful farming experiences.
2. Articles are selected on the sale criteria of usefulness of information for the farmers.
3. Farmers are trained through workshop in writing articles.
4. The major focus is on sustainable agriculture.

The noble experiment is an effort to highlight knowledge and wisdom of farmers. It has created a platform to share their precious experience. The training workshops are held in villages. Besides lectures, the trainers have hands-on writing opportunities. Living in the village provide them opportunity to explore farmers' experiences. Thus, a band of grass-root reporters are being prepared. They have their roots in the villages with interest and experience in agriculture. This is a happy new trend.

INDIGENOUS COMMUNICATION CHANNELS

In every society there are various forms of communication among people. Some channels and forms of communication are deeply rooted in the culture and preserved traditionally from generation to generation. Such channels are called as indigenous traditional folk media. They serve various social needs of the community. They are direct, face to face and linked with emotions and values of people. Thus, they are quite powerful in raising consciousness of people. They are cheap and do not require external resources. Examples of Indigenous communication channel may include various social gatherings like feasts, village meetings, spontaneous gathering at tea shops, festivals, fairs, story telling, magic shows, dances, songs, oral narrations, etc. Mundy and Compton (1991) have stated that indigenous communication can take many forms including the six given below :

Folk Media

Folk media are indigenous equivalents of mass media. They are used primarily for entertainment, but they can also promote educational values and help in cultural continuity. They include festivals, plays and puppet shows, dance, song, story telling, poetry, debates.

Indigenous Organisation and Social Gatherings

Indigenous organisations include religious groups, village meetings, irrigation associations, mothers, clubs and loan association.

Deliberate Instruction

Parents teach children, crafts people instruct apprentices, elders guide young people and adolescents undergo initiation rites. Many societies have traditional religious schools.

Record

Many societies keep records in written, carved, painted or memorized forms.

Unstructured Channels

Indigenous communication occurs in many settings like talk at home and at the well, in the fields and on the road, in tea house and coffee house, in the chief's house and at the market and wherever people meet and talk. This communication is not organised or orchestrated but spontaneous and informal. Communication does not have to be intentional. A farmer may see a neighbour's bumper crop and conclude its usefulness.

Special Features of Indigenous Communication Channels

1. They are precious source of traditional wisdom. Indigenous communication forms contain valuable cultural knowledge on a variety of useful themes including vocations, natural resource, philosophy in understandable terms.
2. They are capable of raising public consciousness. As indigenous channels are popular and linked with the emotions and aspirations of people, they have great appeal to the masses. Messages of development can be effectively communicated in local idioms, proverbs and symbols. In past, messages of high yielding varieties were communicated to the people through folk songs in India.
3. They have both entertainment and information value. They are already popular sources of entertainment. So they naturally attract attention and thus information is easily communicated to those who are otherwise not reached through modern media.
4. They are people oriented. They involve people both as resource (talents) and audience. People have control over it.
5. They are credible and culturally compatible. As people believe them and can understand them easily, they are acceptable in rural society.
6. They are quite inexpensive and informal. As the indigenous channels do not require outside resources, they are economic without much formality.

Examples of Traditional Folk Media in India

Traditional Folk Theatre/Rural Drama

Jatra (Bengal)
Burra Katha (Andhra Pradesh)
Ram Leela (U.P)
Bidesia (Bihar)
Jat Jatin (Bihar)

Puppetry

Sutradharika (String puppet)
Putalnautch (Road puppet)
Chhaya Putli (Shadow puppets)
Glove Puppets

Oral Literature-cum-Musical Forms

Alha (Bihar, U.P)
Baul (W.B)
Bhatialiali (W.B)
Bihu (Assam)
Gurba (Gujarat)

Fairs and Festivals

Social rituals, ceremonies, gatherings, etc.
Ganpati Utsav, Rathyatra, Dussehra, Ram Navami

Folk Dances

Bhangra, Gidha, Garva

Traditional Youth Clubs

Ghotul (Munda), Gitiora (Munda), Rang Bhang (Bhotia), Dhum Kuri (Oraon) and Morang (Nagas).

Rituals/Symbols/Motifs

Rangoli, Alpna, Madhubani painting

Use of Indigenous Communication in Extension

Indigenous channels have attracted attention of social scientists as diffusion studies indicated importance of opinion leadership and inter-personal networks. Of late, studies have indicated how new varieties of agriculture were adopted by the farmers without help or deliberate efforts of extension workers. Peer group, village elders, youth groups, market place and ceremonial occasions may easily be used to disseminate useful information strategically. Experienced farmers can be used as trainees.

USE OF PUPPETS IN DEVELOPMENT — A CASE

Though puppets have largely been used for entertainment, there is a successful case of its application in communicating developmental messages. Shanker Singh, a community worker in Social Work Research Centre, Tilonia, Rajasthan (A reputed voluntary organisation) used puppets to create awareness and mobilize people for development. It was possible for him to use recognisable characters, local gossips and real life events to drive points home in interesting manner. The villagers enjoyed the stories conveyed through puppets. Shanker Singh was very much in demand in villages etc. pull crowds and appeal for donations or good road or solve such other problems. He innovated a character. 'Jokhim Chacha', supposedly a 300 years old man who would call anyone a child and chide even elders and authorities. Thus, even sensitive topics were handled amicably without hurting anyone. After all Jokhim Chacha was such elderly.

NEW COMMUNICATION TECHNOLOGIES

New communication technologies have emerged in past two decades such as microcomputers, cable TV, Teleconferencing, teletext and desktop publishing are all examples of advances in communication technology. Many of these technologies use miniature forms of erstwhile larger equipments and offer opportunities of interaction viz. Computer-assisted-instruction, interactive video, compact-disc read-only memory (CD-ROM).

Micro-computers

Computers are classified as mainframes, mini computer and micro computers based on their power, speed of executing a set of instructions and the amount of memory available to store data as well as the degree of inter connectivity the computers offer. Mainframe computers were large and costly. Mini computers are less powerful. Microcomputers are based on micro-chips technology. In India micro computers were introduced in 1978. There are many uses of micro computers as given below:

1. It can process all kinds of information and keep as record to be retrieved as and when needed. It can be a repository of various experiences, cases and research information on required topics. A training institution may keep all its record on training courses and trainees for evaluation and reporting. Such information can be used for monitoring purposes by headquarters.
2. It can publish information material at reasonable cost for extension purposes.
3. Micro-computers can communicate with each other if linked together. With the help of certain hardwares i.e. micro-computer, modem (a device which translates computer signals into phone signals and *vice-versa*), a printer, telephone and mocrowave or satellite, computers can enable users to access the data from anywhere through micro-computer and phone.

Nieviwsma (1984) has reported that AGNET, a computer network designed for use by extension agents, farmers and extension clientele was introduced in North Dakota Extension Service in USA in 1977. AGNET is used for problem-solving, information sharing and communication. Farmers can get answers to their everyday management problems through problem solving function. Information sharing keeps extension agents update on information. An electronic mail system serves the communication function by speeding up distribution of messages among staff.

4. Accounting function can be greatly facilitated by use of computer by designing more detailed financial record in less time.

Video Text

Video text or view-data is an electronic text service transmitted from central computer to home TV set via telephone network or cable system. It is interactive in the sense that viewer has option to access desired data. Video text and teletext have common features and uses except the mode of transmission which in case of teletext is through broadcast system. It is one way system. Components of video text system are as given below :

Host Computer System

Each video text system has a host computer. The size of computer system varies according to number of users, amount of storage and speed of access required.

Composing and Data Entry

The process through which text are composed and entered into video text system.

Transmission System

It consists of transmission via telephone or cable line.

Display System

A video monitor specially designed for the purpose are used to deliver video text data.

User Retrieval System

Users have a decode to retrieve information from the system. It may be a terminal key board to select pages or communicate with the system.

Electronic Mail (E-Mail)

Electronic mail or E-mail is a mail system which passes information electronically from sender to receiver. Thus, it is a simple way to communicate between two people through computer. E-mail is like surface mail in which a message or letter is typed into computer and sent to another computer via telephone. The message is stored there until the receiver asks for it. Thus, computer acts here as post office. The message in E-mail can be in one of the many forms from voice to text image or drawing. An E-mail system provides for mail box which user can see by using personal computer and modem connected to telephone. E-mail has following advantages.

- It connects two busy people. The sender may not know where the receiver is located. Sender may refer to user code address which the user may retrieve at convenience.
- It makes communication faster as it eliminates time spent to type, edit, despatch and deliver.
- It is cheaper than sending message by telex or fax.

Interactive Video

Interactive video refers to a video system which is a combination of computer and video. It uses multi-media approach i.e. text, stills, video, audio, slides, overheads, etc. The messages stored in various forms are retrieved by user according to choice. The users response to the system determine the path to be followed. There are various levels of interactive video as given below (Fort, 1984).

Level-I : The simplest design consists of video player-tape or disc and a television set or monitor. The user operates the player to review material. The amount of interactivity is limited by the function of the player. A remote control is included for ease of operation.

Level-II : In this level, video disc player alongwith an internal micro-processor is included, which is programmed to perform certain playback sequences and respond to viewer's choices during the programme. The programme control is encoded on the disc.

Level-III : It involves a computer which responds to the user's input. The computer controls all other devices such as video-tape or video disc player and audio devices. This level of interactivity provides all the benefits or Computer Aided Instruction (CAI) such as branching, user-controlled pace, lesson management, record keeping and feedback. This level can involve special accessories such as tough screens, light, pens, bar code readers and devices which allow simulated equipment adjustment. According to Hussey (1985), there are three major functions of extension viz. Information delivery, education delivery and problem-solving. Interactive video can provide information of choice or train farmers in pesticide application technique or help in identifying which fertilizer to use for particular crop. It is most useful medium for training providing individualised instruction at one's own pace. If used properly Interactive video can be most cost-effective than traditional one-to-one training.

Apparao (1990) listed the following advantages.

- There is no need for teacher.
- It has self-paced learning.
- It has powerful video and sound.
- It has multi-media effect.

- It allows for interactive learning.
- Delivery costs of multi-media are greatly reduced.
- It has 3-D graphic simulation, real life situations, etc.
- It is long lasting.

Teleconferencing

Teleconferencing is interactive group communication. Teleconferencing refers to a system for creating dialogue between geographically dispersed participants. Advances in telecommunication and computer have made it possible to hold meetings without travelling to long distances. Teleconferencing can help physically distant people talk together.

Types of Teleconferencing

Audio Teleconferencing : The simplest form of teleconferencing is the use of amplified speaker phones to join groups of people at each end of a telephone conference. High quality audio reception and transmission can be achieved.

Computer Conferencing : Computer conferencing is a variation of electronic mail which enables multiples users, geographically isolated to carry out dialogue. Information is transmitted through a computer with an elaborate store-and-forward message handling system. In a computer conference participants need not be involved simultaneously. One participant may send a message at any time and it may be read by others whenever they have time. A computer conference is basically a group activity. A group can select to participate. Each participant may put their message and read others' contribution. Messages are stored, thus allowing those who join late to retrieve and catch up with the conference.

Video conferencing is like television.

Advantages of Teleconferencing

It allows for increased participation and dialogue between the group members.

Cost and time spent in travel is minimised.

Non-intensive and focussed dialogue is possible.

Planning Communication Strategy

Planning refers to the process of determining appropriate future action through a sequence of choices. Planners seek to organise resources (things, people, money) into action in order to get anticipated results. Middelon defined planning as application of theory to reality in order to decide what to do where and how. Communication is also a resource to be utilized in pursuit of development. Like all resources, communication resources have to be used efficiently. There are an array of communication media available today. The trends in development of communication technologies offer options for a variety of media ranging from audio-tape, flipchart, poster, traditional forms, video, computer to television, radio, satellite linked television, etc. Thus, these media forms require organisation and allocation of resources for training, staff, infrastructure etc. concept of communication planning has become more urgent now in view of the increasing availability of communication media and complexities of media organisation.

Communication Strategy

A strategy refers to some design to use resources (power) to attain given goals through certain instrumental actions. A communication strategy is a set of decisions concerning communication directly instrumental to the attainment of goals. It answers to the questions who is to communicate what to whom what for and how. There are six major steps in formulating communication strategies, viz. Analysis of audience, formulation of communication goals, selection of communication methods and media, message design, planning communication activities and evaluation, as given below :

Analysis of Audience

The first step in formulating communication strategy is to analyse audience with whom we want to communicate. In order to design our message and select media knowledge about their values, present understanding and practices regarding the topic are essential. Besides, reach of different media and their popularity should be analysed. If we could know how do people receive, accept information usually, it would be easy to decide appropriate approach. Effective communications uses recognisable scenes local terms, popular character and easy-to-follow format. Audiency study help to categorise people on the basis of their distinguishing features.

Formulation of Communication Goals and Objectives

Goal refers to the outcome with time frame. Goals are broad in nature.

Objectives indicate direction work or specific changes expected. Communication objectives related to mental process. They imply behavioural changes in terms of information, motivation, practices adopted, etc. Such explicit description of behavioural outcome help in designing matching strategies and evaluate them later.

Selection of Communication Methods and Media

An extension worker must be guided by certain criteria to choose appropriate method and media in order to enhance effectiveness of work. Is there some rule? There is no patent formula as such. It depends on a number of considerations and of course some common sense. Farmers often prefer their neighbours and friends as source of new information. Many a time important technologies have been adopted by farmers without the help or support from extension or research personnel. Thus, there is need to understand farmers' sources of communication. Some of the important factors affecting selection of communication channel have been elaborated below :

Audience Characteristics

Choice of methods and media vary according to background. Socio-economic variable like age, farm-size, language capability, education etc. determine access to media of communication. Large farmers possess radio, and television sets and may also subscribe to magazines or newspapers. Literacy is key determinant in planning use of printed materials.

Audience Size

The number of people to be reached is a major consideration for choosing individual group or mass methods.

Purpose

The objective of extension teaching whether to inform, create interest, teach skill or increase understanding would determine the choice. Knowledge and understanding can be enhanced through lecture, group discussion and meetings whereas skill can best be taught through method demonstration, video and practical exercises. Critical thinking can be developed through problem-solving, group discussion and workshop.

Time

How much time is available to prepare materials? How long particular method needs to be used? These considerations are important because printing leaflets or producing specific video programme take long time.

Cost
The cost involved in producing materials or using a method need to be assessed in relation to number of people to be covered effectively. Budget available for the purpose as well as availability of matching services should be taken in view.

Size of Staff
Number of people working with you determine whether methods involving intensive work like exhibition should be undertaken or not.

Characteristics of Each Method/Medium
Each method and medium have particular characteristics that make it better suited to inform or motivate or train. Like result demonstration provides local proof and builds confidence in technology. Method demonstration teaches skill. Mass media can create interest in the topic whereas visual aids can support lectures, meetings and group-discussion. Audio tapes are good to provide dramatized information. Video-tape and films show complex processess in interesting manner. Use of transparency can enliven instruction by providing systematic progression or ideas. Printed materials have creditability and reference value. In general, individual methods are good to encourage participation. Group and mass contact methods reach large audience.

Multi-media Strategies

Studies have proved that there is no one best medium of communication. No single medium can effectively meet the goals because each medium has its own characteristic strengths and weaknesses. However, combination of media can help in complementing and supplementing each other. The strength of certain media can help to compensate the weaknesses of other media in combination. Some of the well-tried media combinations include use of mass media with inter-personal channels such as information disseminated through radio can be well supported by discussion among listeners of rural listeners club called as rural radio forum. The difficulties of language and abstraction of ideas can be overcome in this way if the leader helps in relating information with local examples.

In Peru, the strategy of communicating agricultural information to farmers included use of flyer with radio programmes, reinforcement radio programmes, learning guide, group-training demonstration and individual training. Here flyers constituted basic text on technologies with well illustrated graphics. These contents were explained through radio programmes in step by step manner. These instructional radio programmes were supplemented by reinforcement radio programmes, containing suggestions and alternative, as a result of responses received from the field. Learning guides were printed and distributed for each crop in order to see details after listing to radio programmes. The farmers attended training programmes and they also had opportunities to participate in individual training and see demonstrations. Thus, there were enough opportunity to get feedback through such individual contact. Such feedback also helped radio station in redesigning programmes with appropriate cases and examples.

Another communication project supported by Food and Agricultural Organisation in Peru, used video in combination with printed guides and discussions led by the extension agents followed by demonstration and practice. While video was the major medium to provide information specific to the target group. In order to make terms and process clear, printed guides were prepared for both learners and extension agents to help at the time of viewing. Extension agents had instructions to stop video at designated points while playing it before the farmers so that farmers can discuss their doubts and problems. Required implements and inputs were kept ready so that extension agents can demonstrate the practices to the farmers. Farmers got chance to practise also and learn the required skills. Thus, a series of videos were produced to meet information and skill needs of farmers.

Message Design

After selecting a set of methods and media, one must decide about matching messages for each media so that desired objectives are achieved. Message design refers to decisions about amount and level of information, sequence, language pace, choice of symbols and mode of presentation. Messages need to be treated according to audience characteristics and type of media being dealt with. Large farmers need information on latest technology whereas farmers with small holdings can make use of messages which are less complex and more economical. Messages affect people most if they are designed on the basis of audience needs and preferences. Thus, it is essential to test messages on sample of audience to make sure that audience perceive them as relevant. It is often assumed that illustrations or photographs will enhance effectiveness of written material. However, experiences have shown that farmers with little exposure to written materials perceive visual symbols differently.

Formulation of Communication Plan

In order to use communication media various activities need to be planned in phases like staff recruitment, training of staff, production of materials, evaluation of material, distribution of material and co-ordination of various activities. Work-schedule need to be formulated to orchestrate various activities. Communication plan should indicate schedule of work in sequence to help in monitoring as given below :

Calendar of Activities (1996-97)

	Months											
Activities	J	F	M	A	M	J	J	A	S	O	N	D
Identification of technology	<---	----	--->									
Base line research		<---	----	----	--->							
Produce radio lesson					<---	----	--->					
Broadcasting							<---	----	----	--->		
Production of literature					<---	----	--->					
Demonstration							<---	----	----	--->		
Distribution of literature							<---	----	----	--->		
Final evaluation										<---	----	--->

Evaluation

All communication materials must be pre-tested for attractiveness, understanding and acceptance. Field testing determines whether these elements are present and how to include them in final product. Evaluation is needed with regard to content and manner of presentation. Representative sample of audience should be consulted to evaluate communication. Overall communication strategy should be evaluated for its effectiveness.

REFERENCES

Anonymous (1992). Spreading News and Literacy in Nepal — The Batabaran Newspaper. *Development Communication Report* No. 79, 1992, 4, pp. 16-17.

Colle, R. (1975). ACT : *A New Kind of Communication, Educational Broadcasting International,* The British Council, Vol. 8.

Faludi, A. (1973). *A Reader in Planning Theory.* Pergamon Press, Oxford, U.K.

Fort, W. (1984). A Primer on Interactive Video. *A. V. Video,* pp. 29-41.

Gupta, V.S. (1984). Farm Journalism — the Indian Perspective, paper presented at the National Seminar on Agricultural Journalism Problems and Prospects held on March 27-29, 1984 at G.B. Pant University of Agriculture & Technology, Pantnagar.

Hynka, O. (1979). Four single page learning model, *A.V. Instruction,* April 1979.

Kumar, B. and Singh, K. (1991). Developmental use of video — Some experience In the book, *Video for Rural Development* (Eds) Hansra, B.S. and Mathur, P.N., Classical Publishing Co., New Delhi.

Mundy, P. and Crompton, L. (1991). Indigenous communication and indigenous knowledge, *Development Communication Report,* 74 (3), p. 1-3.

Malhan, P.N. (1977). Where is rural press, *Vidura,* 14(2), 1977.

Nieuwsma, Lyonette (1984). AGNET-increasing its effectiveness, *Journal of Extension* May-June, Vol. 22, pp. 11-15.

Verma, R. (1984). Agricultural Reporting in Kerala, National Seminar on Agricultural Journalism : Problems and Prospects held at G.B. Pant University of Agriculture and Technology, Pantnagar from March 27-29, 1984.

Quebrol, N. (1983). Quebrol and Middelton, Some thoughts on Development Communication, Past, Present and Future, *DCR* No. 43, Sep. 1983.

4

TRAINING FOR HUMAN RESOURCE DEVELOPMENT

OVERVIEW

Training is an essential part of extension work in order to develop competence of clients.Training is a sequential activity demanding systematic planning, execution and follow-up. New concepts in training viz. andragogy, experimental learning, learning strategy, micro-lab, etc. provide new approaches to enhance training outcome. Farmers training has received important place in extension programmes. There are a number of institutions dealing with farmers training in India. Selection and training of rural leaders is equally important to multiply extension efforts. A large majority of small, marginal farmers, landless labourers and other resourceless people need to be organised. Raising their consciousness is not possible through paid extension workers alone. It is here that voluntary leaders should be utilized. Finally, regular training or extension personnel is needed. Co-incidentally, a vast training infrastructure has come up, of late, in India.

Training is a powerful tool in the hands of development professional to catalyse human resources. Extension education puts emphasis on developing the quality of life of people in rural areas by strengthening local leadership, self reliance and effective use of indigenous resources. It is here that training can be of immense help. Training of farmers, leaders and extension personnel is needed on continuous basis.

CONCEPT OF TRAINING

Training refers to an act, process or method of one who trains. Training indicates a planned activity to which a person is subjected to induce learning. Training aims at behavioural changes to be used in life or vocation. It has a sense of immediacy about application.

Lynton and Pareek (1967) stated that training consists largely of well organized opportunities for participants to acquire necessary understanding and skill. Training aims at lasting improvement on the job. The kind of education we call as training is not far knowing more but behaving differently.

Strayton (1986) defined training as the acquisition and development of those knowledge, skills, techniques, attitudes and experiences, which enable an individual to make his most effective contribution to the combined efforts of the team of which he is a member.

ILO (1986) defined training as activities which essentially aimed to provide attitude, knowledge and skills required for employment in a particular occupation or a group of occupations for exercising a function in any field of economic activity.

Iffner and Douds (1989) viewed training as development and delivery of information that people will use after attending the training. Effective training requires that you have a clear picture of how the trainees will need to use information after training. This also requires that people practice what they have learnt before they apply it after training.

Thus, the above definitions point to some commonalities about training, as given below :

— Training is planned and purposeful instruction. It is non-formal of semi-structured in nature.
— Training aims to improve performance of participants so that they can contribute to effectiveness of the group or organization they belong.
— Training is linked with here and now (present) affairs and requires immediate application to be useful.

In brief, training is an instrument to induce change in behaviour of individuals for personal social or organisational effectiveness. Training is basically adult learning activity.

What Training can do ?

— Training can help people to develop job related skills and a

with change in organisation.
- It can develop self-awareness, inter-personal skills, achievement motivation and such other behavioural attributes.
- It can orient people to get equipped for higher responsibilities.
- It can help in creating professionalism and learning culture in organisations.
- It can update people with current changes in technologies.

Limitations of Training

- Training by itself cannot ensure learning unless participants are motivated.
- Training alone cannot bring changes in organisation even if the participant learn new skills. They require facilities and support from work organisation to apply new knowledge.
- Training is not one shot affair. A person requires many exposures and at different stages in career life.
- Training is not solution to problems other than lack of competencies. Training can bring changes in attitudes, skills and knowledge.

Training versus Education

'Training' and 'education' though look alike, often, they have both commonalities and differences. Education is vertically focussed as it aims to prepare people for future roles. In higher education, students are taught courses which they may use in future. To the contrary, training is meant to provide knowledge and skills which people can apply in job. Contents of training are focussed on the immediate needs at the work-place. Contents or subject-matter areas covered in education are broad in nature so that students can gain general understanding and skills to adapt in society or get absorbed in jobs. Education in general and higher education in particular emphasise on development of attitudes and knowledge. No doubt, skills are also imparted to some extent. However, the aim of training is to provide job-skills to improve job performance. Thus, it is said that education is generally for knowing more whereas training is for behaving differently. Formal education is more rigid and structured but training is non-formal and flexible in nature. Even though differences between education and training look wider, there are exceptions too. Education today is changing its nature and losing its classical distance from work-place. There are many educational institutions which are focussing contents on specific job.

How can Training bring Change ?

There is always some criticism about training that it does not usually lead to change. Training cannot necessarily lead to change unless due care is taken to bring desirable change. Some of the important guidelines have been discussed below :

Motivation for Training
Training in vaccum will not produce change. People do not necessarily learn better by attending top-notch training programme. Motivation is an important pre-condition for training. Training must be rewarding in work organisation People want to learn new things if there is discrimination between ineffective and excellent work.

Commitment at the top
Do the top bosses take training seriously. Commitment , presence and expectations of top officials send positive signal down the ladder and enhance participation.

Approach of Training
No doubt interest of participants in the course depends on trainers and their approach to training. Adult learners need respect, consideration of their experience as resource and involvement in decision making. It is about time that traditional approach of experts is done away with. New trainers should become facilitator and resource person to assist in designing experiences that improve performance. Thus, emphasis should now be on individuals strengths and weaknesses and provision for maturing help. Trainees should participate in choosing contents methods activities and use of time.

Co-operation between Work Organisation and Training Institution
Training alone cannot help in bringing change. Equally important is the help and support of work organisation for creative suitable enviornment and facilities to apply new learning . Training must be rooted in local resource, problems and talents. There should be similarity between work environment and training environment so that transfer of learning is natural. Training cannot be effective in insulated

and laboratory like atmosphere.

TRAINING PROCESS

Training has been conceived as a process consisting of three phases, viz. pre-training, training and post-training.

Pre-training

This is preparatory phase prior to actual training. It involves planning of training. A training organisation has to assess individual need for training and decide appropriate course content as well as methods. Arrangements to select participants, inform about course-details and make necessary preparations are completed during this phase.

Training

The actual implementation of training is done in this phase according to plans drawn before. There are many different activities executed simultaneously like reception of trainees, lodging, boarding, organisation of instruction, field trip and monitoring. Due care needs to be taken to create a relaxed atmosphere for the participants to interact freely and practise new skills. A good rapport with participants, personal attention and feedback ensure interests and enthusiasm of participants.

Post-training

Training does not really end with a course. Post-training test, measurement of impact and follow-up of participants at work place are important elements of good training. Good organisations prepare report and put efforts to bring improvements in training on the basis of evaluation.

Steps in Training

There are four major steps in training, viz. training needs assessment, training programme development, training implementation and evaluation and follow-up.

Training needs Assessment

Assessment of individual needs for training is first step toward designing courses relevant to participants and their organisations. Training needs refer to the gap in individual's current level of abilities and those desired to perform effectively. Training needs are expressed in terms of gaps or deficiencies in attitude knowledge or skills. There are a number of methods to assess training needs such as interviews, questionnaire, observation focus group, informal talk, etc. Some common methods have been elaborated below :

Personal Interview

Individuals are contacted personally at their conveniences and relevant questions are asked in relaxed manner. Efforts are made to build rapport, clarify purpose and proceed in natural conversational format. The question should address current work-behaviour, problems, personal strengths, weaknesses and preferences for training. This method is costly and time consuming . Alternatively group interviews may be conducted and diverse viewpoints may be clarified. The opinion of different segment of population can thus be collected without spending much time.

Questionnaire

Printed or cyclostyled set of questions arranged in logical order are mailed to the concerned individuals for quick response. It is economic to get response from people located at distance. Questionnaires, however, require careful wording and formulation of statements that stimulate desirable responses. Specific and close-ended questions that require choosing response from options provided, are easy to tabulate. Questionnaires should be self-explanatory. The questions must relate to nature of works, areas in which individuals are deficient, level of difficulties in performance, reasons and problems of poor performance, type of knowledge and skills required.

Observation

Training needs can be assessed by observing people at work. Every task requires a number of steps to be completed with efficiency. Direct observation of these steps with the help of structured schedule can provide evidence of current abilities observations can be supplemented with discussion.

After collecting data on training needs, some criteria have to be decided for indicating training priority. All needs cannot be considered simultaneously. Thus, critical needs have to be identified on the basis of number of people having particular need, extent of difficulty in performing an important task, extent of contribution of a task to overall production, etc. Training needs assessment and provides rational basis to design relevant training.

Training Programme Development

In order to develop good training, objectives should be specified. Objectives serve as basis to decide about content and methods of training. Finally strategy of training is formulated combining content, methods and approach of implementation together . Training objective is also called as learning objectives as it specifies what learner should achieve at the end of a training. The objectives mentioned in terms of behaviour are attitude, knowledge or skill. Good objectives are stated in specific terms so that behavioural outcomes can be measured.

Example : At the end of the course participants can

— Write script for video production

— Operate video-camera

Objectives provide basis to decide the content. Depending on the level of participants, content areas are identified. Knowledge required to inculcate desired ability, can be decided by the experts. Contents must be arranged in sequence from simple to complex order. Theoretical concept should be followed by practice. The pace of delivery and need for repetition or review can be adjusted according to the ability of participant. The contents must be organised realistically so that they are covered within time frame.Variety helps to keep interest. On the basis of understanding about participants background and objectives setforth, training methods and activities should be chosen. There are various training methods in use. There is need for using methods which stimulate participants involvement in the process of learning. Distinctive features of some of the common methods are given below :

Lecture : It is most commonly used method. It is quite useful to pass well sequenced information to a large number of people. There is little or no feedback from the participants because trainer is more keen to present ideas. Participants remain passive most of the times. Lecture can be made lively through well planned theme with examples and stories from real life. Trainer may turn a lecture into discussion by posing a practical problem. Lecture can be quite effective in combination with demonstration.

Discussion : In discussions, experiences of people are used. Every participant is treated as equal and capable of contributing ideas. Use of democratic procedures and close group work enhance feeling of 'we'. It teaches people to tolerate differences of opinion and express once its opinion. Attentive listening and active participation are required all-through. Trainer should guide participants to stay on theme and encourage everybody's active involvement. This method creates motivation and generates new ideas.

Role-Play : Role-Play provides opportunities to participants to act the role of characters assigned by the trainer. There is no advance planning or preparation. Trainer narrates a problem and describes the characters. Participants have to enact simultaneously. Enactment is followed by discussion on observation and self-analysis. It provides a non-threatening environment, free flow of dialogue, and interesting situation. There is high level of involvement. Trainer can skilfully lead the participants to conclusions. Thus this method is full of activity, enthusiasm, sharing and self-directed learning. It is easy to play roles that participants had experienced in past.

Case-study : Case study is ideal method to train participants in problem-solving and decision making. A case should have adequate description of some real situation so as to facilitate discussion and analysis. Participants are required to be active to use their knowledge. It requires ability to diagnose problem and provide solution. A case study may be distributed in the form of tape, video-tape, written case or oral description. Case study provides indirect experience of a given situation. It holds interest and encourages problem-solving.

Brain Storming : The method is used for stimulating creative ideas and problem-solving. There are two phases in brain-storming viz. idea-generation and idea evaluation. It is conducted in non-threatening environment. Every participant is encouraged to offer his ideas. At first there is no judgement or discussion. Only after everyone has offered ideas that all the ideas are grouped and analysed critically to come to conclusion. Trainer simply guides the process, and helps in recording ideas.

Sensitivity Training : It is also known as laboratory training or T-Group (Training Group). It aims to enlighten participants about their own reactions and inter-personal relationship. Training is conducted with 8-10 trainees. Trainers help the group in analysing their behaviour and experiences. Each participant serves as object of study by himself. Use of exercises and instruments involve participants. Individuals become sensitive about their own perceptions and hidden feelings of others. This method is based on the premise that individuals need to understand themselves before establishing satisfactory relationship with others by becoming sensitive to other people's hidden feelings.

Training Camp : Training may be organised in a camp like situation with a very busy schedule of working. The elements of organising community work may also be naturally conducted in field situation. They provide good setting for inculcating skills of team work and joint action.

Field trip : Use of pre-structured field trips may be very much helpful in providing direct experience of actual situation. Opportunities of meeting and talking with those already occupying and exercising leadership functions, visiting their projects and observing their methods of organisation may help in visualising their roles.

Project Work : Involvement of trainees in some on-going projects through working, is quite helpful in acquiring practical skills.

Use of Reading Materials in Training Programme

Reading may facilitate in providing proper perspective on development work. Sometimes folders, bulletins, magazines and newspapers may be displayed at appropriate places which the participants may pick up at leisure time. They may help in inculcation of reading habits. Reading about biographies and deeds of great people, may provide insights and ideas for their own work.

Use of Cultural Programme

Cultural programmes may be used as important training tool for breaking loose the differences and facilitating closer interact. This will not only release creativity but intentional use of such programmes may facilitate better learning of social realities. They may be encouraged to interact themselves.

Knowledge is gained through lecture, reading discussion, etc. whereas skills are imparted through demonstration and practice, mass media, case study and role play help in bringing attitudinal changes. Thus, various activities and blend of lecture, practice, discussion, visits, etc. should be decided to encourage involvement and interest. Training programme should finally state day-to-day activities and details of sessions so that they can be implemented. A number of preparations are required in order to launch the training according to plan training materials, viz. detailed course outline, training notes, programme detailed, visual aids. Logistic arrangements like transport site of training, lodging and boarding, etc. require advance planning.

Training Programme Implementation

In order to execute the programme of training in right earnest, appropriate learning atmosphere should be created as detailed below :

Reception of Trainees

The trainees should be received at the site of arrival and made comfortable. The schedule of training and other required information should be provided.

Registration and Pre-programme Evaluation

Registration of participants and supply of stationeries, viz. name tag, writing pad, training schedule, papers etc. should be done before starting any session. In order to measure effectiveness of training, a pre-evaluation questionnaire should be administered to them.

Introduction of Participants

In order to help the participants become familiar with each other and overcome initial inhibitions, one of the useful methods is microlab. Microlab consists of series of exercises which can provide better understanding of the group, trainers and the training programme.

Building the Training Group

A clear understanding of training activities will help in easing the anxieties. The trainer should establish rapport with all participants. The participants should become a co-operative and harmonious learning group. Trainers should give due importance to knowledge and experience of participants and use them during training.

Monitoring of Programme
Keen observation on participants behaviour and execution of programme would help to see the gaps, if any. Are the participants taking interest ? Do they find content relevant ? Are they satisfied with instruction.

Give and Get Feedback
Trainers should provide feedback on progress of participants in a manner that they can make necessary change, point out the positive development and let them know of the lacunae in a suggestive manner. Trainers should also try to know the participants reactions.

Evaluation

Evaluation means assessment of value of merits of a programme. Evaluation can help in assessing gain in knowledge, skills or attitudes due to training. Reactions of participants can be known. Usefulness of methods and approaches used can be gauged. Above all, overall impact of training on work performance and production can be measured. Evaluation should be done soon before training begins, during the course of training and after the training is over. Pre-training evaluation helps in understanding level of participants at entry point. Observations and data collected during the process of training point out lacunae and merits in implementation of training.Post-training evaluation is meant to measure impact. There are many methods of evaluation viz. pre-post test, oral evaluation, structured observations and skill test, as discussed below.

Pre-post Tests
In order to measure gain in knowledge due to training set of questions are prepared to be administered both before and after training is done. Similar test is provided both the times and results are compared.

Oral Evaluation
In case the number of participants is not very large, it is easy to get reactions of people about different aspects of training. Trainer may

begin with purpose of such exercise so as to stimulate participants to express their reactions. Good aspects, problems and suggestions for improvement of training can be discussed.

Skill Test

In case of skill training it is possible to design tests, exercises with scores allotted for every step of performance. The participants may be given exercises to complete within allotted time period. Experts can observe and judge them.

Reaction Sheet

Relevance of content and methods as well as extent of satisfaction of participants with training may be taken on quick participants reaction sheets. Simple statements may be formulated to encourage spontaneous expression of feeling about training. It is ideal to prepare evaluation report on training incorporating observation and other data with suggestions for modifications.

NEW CONCEPTS IN TRAINING

There are many new concepts emerging which may help in understanding training. Some of them are discussed below.

Andragogy

Andragogy is a term meaning art and science of teaching adults. The growth and development of andragogy has helped in improving teaching of adults. It is based on understanding about adults and their distinctive learning behaviour, as given below :

— Adult learners try to become independent or selfreliant in learning.
— They possess a vast reservoir of experience which can be used as basis for new learning.
— They demonstrate readiness to learn in porportion with their expanding social roles.
— They have a tendency to learn things which can be immediately applied.

Thus, it is clear that adults have sense of autonomy and they select what to learn. Their own individual experiences serves as resource to new learning. They will resist anything which negates their experience and emphasises on complete adherence to set of rules. It naturally follows that trainer of adults need to design training in a manner that participants experiences and feelings find place in training decisions. Adult participant should get opportunity to explore and find out facts for themselves. Such an approach to training, currently in vogue, is known as experiential learning.

Experiential Learning

Experiential learning refers to the type of learning obtained through transformation of experience into knowledge. The learners are encouraged to involve themselves fully into an experience and later reflect and analyse that experience to draw conclusion or knowledge.

Salient Features of Experiential Approach

Trainers share goals of training and involve participants in making decisions about training activities. Participants learn more through group work. Trainers purposively use exercises or problems which involve two or more people in order to encourage team work. Adults learn better by observing others, listening to ideas and comparing self with others. Interaction in group has additional values. Trainers should create positive climate by creating structures and procedures which stimulate free thinking, discussion and exploration. Trainers have to use appropriate communication skills to facilitate learning. Such skills include attending, observing, questioning, paraphrasing and feedback. Role of trainer here is one of facilitator or guide. Trainers settle goals and help in smooth conduct of group work. They intervene to analyse, clarify doubt and draw conclusion. Effective training which follows experiential learning approach involves four major steps viz. experience process, generalisation and application, as detailed below :

Experience

This is the step in which participants get opportunity to engage in experience through case study, role play, demonstration, etc. These activity help in generating data.

Process

After experience, the trainer guides the group to discuss the experience critically. They show individual reactions, feelings and perceptions to analyse the experience. Emphasis is made to see pattern of trends.

Generalisation

Now participants are encouraged to draw conclusion or essence out of the discussions made in the previous step.

Application

The meaning drawn through generalization is now applied to practical problem situations so that they can plan to use their knowledge to work.

Thus, experiential learning cycle helps participants draw meaning out of experience through discussion and analysis. This is quite appropriate for skill training because of the activity provides. Kind of experience which may easily lead participation to reflection, draw conclusion and identify application points.

Concept of Learning Strategy

Traditionally trainers/training managers used to decide the content and methods of training. The focus of training was on trainers and process of training. The learners were in the background. In contrast, learning strategy puts learners in the focus. The learner is the key actor on the scene and trainer a guide/resource/facilitator to manage learning resource to serve the learner. Learners are involved in directing, deciding the content and evaluating own progress. They participate in selection of learning task. Trainers have to keep, space in training for such negotiations to occur. The point of view of learners and their perspectives are discussed at length to generate consensus. This assumes that all the wisdom does not lie with the trainers. A set of alternate resources are made available to choose, selection is made on the basis of progress of learners, their needs, interests and learning style. It requires a variety of modes like self directed learning, team learning, etc.

Co-training/Team Training

Co-training is method of instruction in which two or more trainers plan and conduct training together. In fact, training alone is quite taxing. In order to teach through media, encourage discussion, motivate group-work and create variety, team of trainers can be helpful. It requires co-operation, mental acceptance of each other and complete co-ordination of action during training. Some of essential requirements for an effective training team are as follows :

— Members should have clear sense of the goal to be achieved.
— They plan work ahead of time and know their exact role and time to act.
— They work continuously to support each other.
— They can give and receive feedback freely.
— There is frequent consultation between members and concern for individual as well as team accomplishments.

There are many advantages of co-training besides sharing of responsibility, better management of group process and variety in instruction.The trainers can jointly analyse and evaluate their training for making improvement.

Microlab

Microlab is useful method to overcome initial psychological inhibitions of participants in the beginning of a training. Participants, coming from different places and backgrounds, bring with them expectations and fears of unknown which inhibit their participation in training. Microlab consists of package of exercises which are organised before starting the course. These exercises help the participants to overcome hitch and accept the training in right perspective. An informal atmosphere is created and participants gain understanding of the group and programme. The activities conducted in microlab stimulate interaction. In order to help the participants get introduced to each other informally, they (participants) are grouped in pairs and each one introduces self without using names, designations and places they come from. Participants may form new pairs and share their weaknesses and earnest desires.

FARMERS' TRAINING

Meaning of Farmers' Training

Many a time farmers' training is casually used to indicate sundry extension activities such as meeting, demonstration or field day. However, it is not totally unstructured or informal as some practitioner might assume. Like any other training, Farmers' training is non-formal instructional activity to equip farmers, housewives, village youths or fishermen to improve their abilities to produce better or take informed decision. Rao (1975) gave precise definition by labelling farmers' training as an intensive learning activity for a group of selected farmers assisted by competent trainers to understand and practice the skills required in adoption of new agricultural technologies at a place where appropriate facilities exist and at a time and duration considered suitable by farmers. Thus, farmers' training is not a casual activity. It is systematic and pre-planned affair. The goals of training have to be specific in terms of behavioural changes to be brought. Looking to the needs of target population, objectives, content and methods of training should be decided by the trainers. The target population may be those adults who are engaged in selected vocations or wish to gain entry trainers may be subject-matter experts, experienced farmers, farm leaders or concerned development personnel. The content of farmers' training depends on analysis of needs and preference. While, production technologies constitute major theme of training for farmers, some community related themes may also been included like community health care, social forestry, social organisation, management of youth clubs. Besides , a new wave of thinking is emerging about need of including self and group skills viz. self-awareness, Interpersonal skills negotiation skills, decision making, team work, etc. for the farmers. After all, farmers has to deal with life and he needs skills to operate in ever-changing world. Such courses will support the attempt to develop human resources in the rural areas.

Growth of Farmers' Training in India

Training is indeed a critical need and wise investment to enhance quality of human resource. A rapid review of the evolution of farmers' training in India will provide proper perspective in this regard. The origin of farmers' training can be traced back to the early voluntary works of Yamunapar project of Allahabad Agricultural Institute, Naini, Allahabad, U.P., where concerted efforts were made towards training of extension workers (called as gaon-saathi or village-friends) and farmers. The earliest mention of farmers'and youths' training is found in the rural reconstruction efforts at Shriniketan, West Bengal. The farmers' training during British regime remained largely unorganised and scattered through voluntary efforts. Some efforts had been made under Grow More Food Campaign in the wake of the Second World War in order ot meet the emergency and feed the militia. With the initiation of Etawah Pilot Project, farmers' training received significant attention through organisation of village leaders' training camp, where all aspects of rural development were covered. Farmers' training was given real boost with the launching of the Community Development programme in 1952. Training for the village leaders was an important part of community development programme. The training aimed to broaden the outlook and secure extensive people's participation. In view of greater importance of agricultural production in the Third Five Year Plan, the demand for fuller utilization of progressive farmers had increased. It was decided, therefore, to select progressive farmers and train them at Extension training Centres, Basic agricultural schools and agricultural colleges. It is worthwhile to mention that considerable attention had been accorded to training planning in every IADP districts. Block level training camps were organised for cultivators and village level staff. Training was an essential part of the overall strategy of agricultural development. Farmers' training grew in strength further with the establishment of the first generation State Agricultural Universities (SAUs), Punjab Agricultural University was perhaps one of the first among them (S.A.Us.) to set up Junior Staff School to impart training to the farmers. The other SAUs also came up. Since then Indian Council of Agricultural Research also followed suit by making efforts to keep some farmers' training activities as part of extension role of ICAR Research Institutes or sub-stations.

The new agricultural strategies called High Yielding Varieties Programme gave utmost importance to farmers' training in spreading the package of cultivation practices. Thus, well organised effort of farmers' training began under the much publicised Farmers' Training and Education Programme in 1966-67. The scheme with three major components, viz. Farmers' training, farm-broadcast and functional literacy aimed to increase the abilities of the farmers to understand and use technology through training, information and literacy. Both institutional and non-institutional training were organised for the entire farm-family. Training Camps were conducted in villages through participating teams with the help of audio-visual aids. In nutshell, a comprehensive programme of farmers' training with media and interpersonal group support took off in the country. The turning point and a giant leap in farmers' training came with the establishment of Farm Science Centre or Krishi Vigyan Kendra by the Indian Council of Agricultural Research (I.C.A.R.). The scheme devoted to the vocational training of farmers, farm women, youth and even field level extension functionaries aimed to bridge the technological gap and augment agricultural production. Never ever in the history, such a serious and systematic effort at farmers' training had been made in the country with such sound and time-tested principle of training and development. Disenchantment with green revolution and high technologies demanded strong emphasis on local resources and appropriate technology. In fact, KVK was an organisational innovation overcoming most of lapses of earlier schemes of rural training, viz.technically ill-equipped weak trainers, poor infrastructure, emphasis on theory, irrelevant training courses. The special features of Krishi Vigyan Kendra embodied the best and all the essential components of non-formal education like need-based skill oriented courses, practical training staff, practical training facilities, emphasis on work experience and organisational linkages. KVK movement has grown from strength to strength. The concepts and approaches tried for about two decades now, have almost stabilised.The onset of the Eighth Five Year Plan has witnessed meaningful integration of all the transfer of technology programmes of the ICAR into KVKs with triple functions, viz.farm advisory services-demonstration of latest technology, vocational training of the farmers, farm women, young farmers and field level extension functionaries, and on-farm research/operational research. The KVKs have now spread across the length and breadth of the country. This important scheme has earned respect and repute over the years.

Critical Issues in Farmers' Training

Farmers' training is an emerging area of investment for accelerating transfer of technology from research stations to farmers' fields. There are a number of institutions engaged in the task like state agricultural universities, Departments of Agriculture, voluntary organizations and input agencies. Besides, there are 131 farmers' training centres and about 189 Krishi Vigyan Kendras devoted exclusively to training of farmers, farm women and school drop-outs. The priority has been given to the disadvantaged i.e., small, marginal farmers and landless labourers for training in location specific and economically viable technologies as they could not benefit from the new agricultural technologies. Various studies suggest that small farmers lack adequate irrigation facilities and their resources for use of external inputs are limited. Small and fragmented holdings do not allow use of heavy agricultural implements and machines. Generally illiterate or neo-literate, small farmers are ignorant about various development programmes. Low in aspiration with less or no risk-orientation, they are hesitant in nature. The large scale migration of farmers from rural areas to urban trade centres for employment have grave economic consequences. Besides, wage rates have increased in the villages. More and more women folks have to be involved in farming. In view of such socio-economic and situational pressures, training of farmers have assumed added significance. Experiences in the country indicate gross neglect of human factors in designing such training. Thus, there is need to explore some ways and means to increase effectiveness of training by considering often neglected features of learning by the oppressed. The success of farmers' training is limited largely because of failure of trainers to design practical need-based and skill oriented courses. Two critical and inter-related components of training are content and a process geared to efficient delivery of relevant and effective training. Some hints for action in this regard are given below :

Identification of Felt Needs

In order to decide the contents for training, trainers must move out and see how farmers work. Observe field, tools, resources, situation etc. Discuss problems being faced. A new technique for identifying the needs, 'participatory rural appraisal', is increasingly being used now-a-days. A team of five to seven workers should go to villages and stay there for two or three days. They can prepare the resource inventory of farmers, observe the crops and discuss individual problems with villagers. They may also invite all the villagers including children and women to their camps and cross check the collected data. Identification of group needs may also be done during this session. Villagers may be asked to propose solution of the problems. Training courses based on actual observation, farmers' expectations and diagnosis can serve the needs. Thus, training needs assessment provides information on where training is needed, what the contents of training should be and who among the villagers need training? This assessment is, however, not complete and a few more questions are required to be answered at this stage, namely, where will it be organized, will it be institutional or non-institutional training, are requisite training facilities available, are resource persons of requisite calibre available, and, lastly, what are the likely outcomes of training?

Selection and Motivation of Potential Trainees

Farmers differ in farm size, literacy level, economic conditions, knowledge, comprehension level, resources, etc. Accordingly, they need different kinds of training. It is essential to categorize farmers according to their status and make training groups as much homogeneous as possible. Successful ex-trainees might prove helpful in selection of trainees in the villages. Motivation has direct relation with relative benefits and need fulfilment. Once farmers understand the benefits of training, nothing can stop their participation.

Choice of Appropriate Technology for Training

The trainers usually blame farmers for not adopting the technologies. Farmers in general and small ones in particular have their own limitations. Thus, in choosing technologies for training, one must ensure availability of resources, relative cost, suitability on small holdings, compatibility with social values, etc. Some technologies are easily taken up due to low or no extra investment. Practices like use of mulching for soil and water conservation, appropriate crop rotation and inter-cropping for insects, pests and weed control, ash for mineral supply will have higher degree of adoption among small farmers as against use of sprinkler, drip irrigation system and pesticides. Besides, there is need to encourage technologies which accelerate cooperation and participation of groups. Experiences suggest that trainers should first emphasize on simple and low or no cost technologies with potential for showing results. Trainers need to acquaint themselves well with the resources of communities, local knowledge and practices before planning introduction of particular technology in a training course.

Designing Practical Training Situation

Farmers' training must be designed around sound principles of adult learning. Adults learn new skills best through practice and experience. They get more involved if problems are drawn from their day-to-day experiences. They easily learn new things that they can relate to past experience. Thus, it is essential to create learning environment conducive to farmers by honouring their experiences. Culturally compatible sitting arrangements and simple facilities may work better than classroom like formal situation. Caution must be exercised in deciding duration of sessions. Farmers become easily bored and have very short attention span when they are sitting and listening. Organization of active experiences like demonstration, problem discussion, role-play, can involve trainees and provide opportunity for reflection. Trainers of farmers need added qualification besides technical specialization. Trainers must know local dialect, practices and possess skills in adult teaching. Involvement of successful farmers as resource persons may also be considered. It is essential to talk in local language as far as possible and use colloquial terms and units to help illiterate farmers understand.

Follow-up

Many training courses end up without result because of lack of adequate follow-up support. It requires repeated persuasion, guidance and advice to help the trainees adopt newly learnt ideas/skills. Some Krishi Vigyan Kendras, have formed association of ex-trainees. Farm Science clubs are also organized in villages to help farmers. Trainers also coordinate with bank and other government agencies in helping trainees receive critical inputs. The KVSs also organises meeting of ex-trainees every year to exchange their experiences. Some KVSs send newsletters to ex-trainees every month in simple language. Punjab Agricultural University encourages the trained farmers to organise a club or a discussion group at their villages. Farmers gather once in a fortnight to discuss their farm problems. They provide farmers with the needed technical and organizational support. The progress of trained farmers at their farms is watched carefully. These after-cares are fruitful wherever in practice.

Key-points for making Farmers' Training Effective

— Farmers' training to be effective must be conducted when it is most needed. It is better to synchronise training with phases of production process viz. pre-sowing, irrigation, use of fertilizers.

- Availability of local resources, inputs, preference and practices of farmers should be analysed carefully before designing training courses for farmers. The trainees must identify segment of farmers viz. large or tractor owning farmers or small farmers.
- It is always helpful to have link between training efforts and developmental programmes run by the state government or other agencies in the area to reap full benefits.
- Teaching illiterates, low-literates or neoliterates not quite used to pen and paper way of learning is challenging.Thus, usual methods of class-room teaching will not work. Teaching by doing and learning by doing have to be put into practice. Use of experienced farmers as resource persons may make training more acceptable.
- Training should emulate life. Most successful farmers' training organisations use local songs, conversational formats, discussion of local news and some community work as part of training process. In no case training should become dull and boring.
- Training must be followed by demonstration, discussion in the field or advice to the farmers so as to reinforce the new learning.

TRAINING OF RURAL LEADERS

Every social group has certain people who command respect. They have influence and undisputed following. Their opinions count. They have people flock around them for information, advice or inspiration. Such people, called as leaders, matter a lot to people. If they are somehow linked with development programmes, the task of development would become very easy. All leaders may not be positively inclined towards development. Thus, selection, training and utilization of such individuals require some efforts. Why should we use leaders in extension work ?

Rationale for Training of Rural Leaders

Selection, training and utilization of rural leaders is essential because of the following reasons :

- Extension has a long tradition of using leaders in extension work.

Extension worker as an outsider may not have complete knowledge about different aspects of village community nor they are supposed to have similar perceptions and feeling about village problems as local people may have. Thus, there are good reasons to use such people who belong to the community.

— Leaders by virtue of their influences can convey messages of development more convincingly in the people's language. They can use arguments and styles of presentation most appropriate for the target population. They can also help to get social sanction for development. Besides, they can also serve as mouthpiece of people before extension workers. They can explain elaborately the needs and aspirations of people.

— Number of extension workers is proportionately far less than required. Thus use of leader can help to multiply effects of extension work conveniently and convincingly.

— Leaders can help in enlisting participation of people in programmes of their own development. It is possible to organise people around concrete problems. Leaders can use their influence and skills to bring people together and empower them to take action for their development.

— Villages in India are still haunted by deep rooted beliefs, customs, superstitions and ignorance which influence development negatively. It calls for different types of efforts to overcome social barriers. Leaders, if positively inclined, can play prominent roles in masterminding development in right earnest.

Concept of Leadership

The Greek root of the term leader, is associated with verbs *'archein'* meaning to begin, lead and rule; and *'pratein'* meaning to pass through, achieve and finish. This means that leader is one who begins and work is finished by the followers. The Latin verbs associated with leadership are *'agere'* (to lead/set in motion) and *'gerere'* (to bear) . Thus, leader is supposedly one who exercises influence over others. This influence helps in directing activities of others. Leadership is basically a group phenomenon. A group consists of two or more people who interact together for fulfilment of common goods. In any given group there is pattern of all reactions and interaction among members. Relative strength of attraction or inter-personal relationship of the members of a group determines leadership.

"According to Tead, leadership is the activity of influencing people to co-operate towards some goal which they come to find desirable".

Haiman described leadership as an effort to direct the behaviour of others toward a particular end.

Thus it can be said that —

— Leadership is a matter of influencing people in the group.
— Leader is able to gain co-operation of members in achieving the goal.
— The decision of people to follow the leader is voluntary.

. Leadership is not bossing, commanding or ordering. It is mutually stimulating relationship between leader and the group. While leader is able get the work done, followers are not passive either. Followers' reactions and views exert influence on leader. The fact that leaders exert, does not exclude others from influencing. It is a matter of position or relative strength that one person has more influence.

Existing Pattern of Rural Leadership

There are two broad categories of leader in villages, viz. traditional and emergent leaders. Traditional leaders command influence on the basis of land, wealth or certain inherited status belonging to tradition like caste leaders, land lord, priest. Emergent leaders are those persons who command influence on the basic of their personal qualities, specialization or office of power, political affiliance or such other acquired traits such as progressive farmers, head of village council (panchayat) co-operative or member of a voluntary or political organisation.

Traditional Leader

They are respected because they possess wealth or power to conduct social rituals/ceremonies. Thus, they fulfil social and religious needs of the people. They uphold those values. There are many other terms to indicate various types of traditional leaders as given below :

Caste Leaders

If the influence of some leaders extend to particular caste group, such individuals have interest and active role in social and economic development of their own caste. They are more acceptable by members of their own caste.

Sacred Leader

The term specifically refers to those who officiate in various religious and social ceremonies. They are prominent in sacred or spiritual field such as priests or *ojhas* (exorcists). Such traditional leaders, however, have influence over a section of society. They are characterised by inherited status due to birth in a family. However, their role in development programme can be limited due to their value orientations and partisan interests.

Emergent Leaders

Emergent leaders have come on the rural scene due to new opprortunities available in the villages such as village council (panchayat), co-operatives, voluntary organisations, rural branches of political parties, etc. Emergent leaders are known by different terms as given below :

Personal Leaders
Those leaders who are valued due to their specialized skills such as progressive farmer.

Professional Leaders
They are people who command respect or influence by virtue of their professional status, training, etc. such as village extension worker or village school teacher.

Political Leaders
They are affiliated with an ideology or political party and command respect by virtue of their initiatives in the party.

Social Leaders
Leaders of various social organisations located in the villages,

command influence because of their involvement in development of people.

There are sharp differences in leadership pattern among progressive and non-progressive villages (Reddy and Sahay, 1973). Leadership in non progressive villages is polymorphic in nature i.e. one person is sought for advice on a variety of areas such as cultivation, marriage, official works, etc. In non-progressive villages, leadership is monomorphic or specialized in nature.

Leadership structure in rural India has undergone a sea change during post-independence era. The planned national development efforts, democratically elected governments and policy of involving people in institutions of development, have created consciousness at the village level. The strong hold of traditional caste-oriented leadership is on the wane. Many youths from backward caste have emerged prominently, of late, in villages due to opportunities available in panchayat, co-operative, village schools and voluntary organisations.

Selection of Leader

Potential leaders can be selected on the basis of their attribute. Leaders for extension work must possess a blend of following quantities :

Volunteer
The incumbent must come out on his/her own to work for the cause of the community. In every society there are people with altruistic tendency.

Secular
People with partisan interest cannot serve for the cause of the whole village.

Democratic
Basic belief in individual supremacy and need for equal involvement of one and all in development programmes is a must.

Honesty
Sense of honesty and reliability builds trust for the leader in a group.

Positive Enthusiasm
An abounding sense of joy and natural interest in development work

sustains involvement of leader in hours of stress.

Friendliness
Good leader feels deeply for those with whom he works. Friendly attitude inspires others to seek his contact.

Scientific Outlook
Development work demands appreciation for breaking away from shackles of irrational beliefs and systems of living.

A number of other attributes have been mentioned by various experts such as intelligence, tact, patience, poise, sense of humour, health, fairness, dependability, originality, sincerity, loyalty, integrity, vision, ethics, perseverance, courtesy, sympathy, industriousness, fearlessness, impartiality, emotional stability, decisiveness, technical mastery, teaching, skills etc. However, it is helpful for a potential leader to be a good experienced farmer himself to be able to command natural influence. Understanding and concerns for the problems of the village can be a motivation force to work further. A study by Verma and Lewis (1978) demonstrated the following qualities in successful community development leader (community aid).

— Highly motivated with positive attitude towards community improvement.
— High school or college educated in a professional education.
— Influence both within and outside the community to be able to take complex projects involving external resources.
— A correct concept of his/her role in community development, namely motivating, organizing education, leading and serving people.
— A proper work style of involving key community elements.

How to Identify Potential Leaders ?

There are many ways to locate people with desirable qualities and potential to play leadership role, as given below :

Discussion
An opportunity for discussion on real issue gets people in action giving expression to their knowledge, group skill and power of conviction. This is said to be a live laboratory to see display of power and

influence in natural condition.

Workshop/Problem Solving

Problem solving or working on real issues facing the community gives people chance to exercise their insights, skills of problem solving, knowledge of the subject and group process. Team work, decision making and other managerial abilities are also expressed.

Participative Observation

Eventhough observation is part of both discussion and workshop methods, leaders can be selected through close observation in the community by observer being a part of the scene for a period of time. This provide him enough data regarding conditions of the community, opportunities of leadership and skills.

Sociometric Technique

The term 'Sociometry' refers to the pattern of attraction among members of a group. Sociometric technique is meant for determining the extent to which individuals are accepted in a group. This helps in revealing the relationship structure within a group. The technique can be applied if all the members of the group know each other well. In order to seek preference for leader the specific context (situation) is explained to each member and he is asked to give a number of preference (say first, second and third) alongwith rating. Thus people are given a situation narrating whom do you consult from your village if you have problems regarding cultivation, name three persons from community in order of preference. Sociometric score is calculated by multiplying number of incoming choices for each person and total of scores obtained in terms of preferences. Thus, individuals are ranked on the basis of sociometric score.

Training of Village Leaders

The task of developing villages cannot be achieved without trained democratic leaders with secular and social outlook. While potential leaders should be selected from the village communities concerned, they would require training to play enabling role. Training of potential leaders is essential for strengthening local initiative for development. This will accelerate implementation of on-going efforts. Training, however, should not be thought as one-stroke affair. It would rather be a continuous process although various levels of training may be designed. However, to start with the goal of training would be as below:

— To motivate local leaders to commit themselves for the cause of development.
— To create general awareness in them about the problems of villages, current approaches of development, national policy, organisation etc.
— To indicate in them basic skills of communication and group work.
— To provide them knowledge and skills in technical subject matter area relevant to the programme.

Content Areas for Leaders' Training

The following four contents areas may be considered for organisation of leaders' training.

General Awareness related with Village Work
Leaders must operate out of a clear vision of the goal of rural development. They need to understand the existing approaches of development, organisational structure, problems, regulations, etc. They should also know various alternative approaches and consequences of changes taking place in social economic, political, cultural and technological sectors.

Motivational Component
Motivation is key to committed work. All religious or political organisations infuse volunteers with motivation. Leaders must draw the source of inspiration from their basic needs, scripture, history, tradition and culture. An indirect curriculum is thus essential to inspire people to take the cause of development as their personal goal out of choice, this may be interwoven in the form of songs cultural activities, method of working, daily rituals, etc. Besides, discussion on life works and ideologies of great men can motivate leaders. People must be inspired to see reasons to undertake an apparently non-remunerative challenging task of voluntary service. They must find meaning in the work.

Basic Skills and Group Work
Leaders requires basic skills in writing, speaking, arithmetic, record

keeping, etc. Besides they need skills in organising meeting, conducting group discussions, working in team, community organisations implementation of programmes, seeking help from external agencies.

Technical Subject-matter

Depending upon the interest of the incumbents, nature of development work, some technical knowledge and skills should also be provided to them to enable their expertise in the field. This will give them an edge to demonstrate, advise and lead.

Essential Features of Leaders Training

The training to fulfil the goals mentioned in the proceeding context must adopt approach essential for bringing desired impact :

— The leaders must be trained through a process of dialogue or group interaction rather traditional lectures and notes, in order to inculcate right skills for facilitating participative leadership.
— The training should create an open and participative atmosphere. There should be enough opportunity to reach decisions through critical discussion among trainers and trainees with open mind and not take anything for granted.
— The training should help in acquiring and reinforcing values like justice, equality, honesty, solidarity through day-to-day working.
— The ways of organising training must reflect the value to be taught and imbibed during the sessions. It should be participatory, non-hierarchical and democratic in every aspect of its organisation. Trainees must have a say in most aspects of the organisation.
— The discussion and analysis should be based on the realities expressed by the participants in their life and work. They should begin with the known and lead to unknown.
— The training venue and set-up should be realistic, closer to the village life so that they can relate with their own situation.
— Practical involvement in work, worship, site visits, role playing and, cultural programmes should be used more frequently.
— The period of training may vary from a day to a few weeks depending upon the intent. In the beginning intensive training of long duration may be desirable for preparing adequately in the techniques of organisations, group working and practical vocational skills. However, the training for development of leadership would

be continuous affair to be imparted from time to time, though in varying forms.

TRAINING OF EXTENSION PERSONNEL

Extension personnel are vital link between research organisations and farmers. Agricultural development today calls for well trained extension personnel who can keep pace with changes. In India, there is tremendous change in economic policy, technologies and even extension programmes. Training is important to help the extension personnel to meet the challenges education faces now than ever. The regional imbalances in agricultural production, vast majority of small and marginal farmers, large track of diverse risk-prone areas and above all, fragile natural resource demand extension service with sensitivity for the poor and marginalised. At the same time, there is need for value-added products of high quality export.

Rationale for Training

Extension personnel need to update their knowledge and skills continuously of effectively serve the clientele. Thus, the importance of training as an indispensable instrument of human resource development cannot be ignored. Regular training of extension personnel should help in developing their capacity in the following ways :

— Training should provide role clarity, sense of purpose and belonging to the organisation of which a person is part. People perform better if they are oriented from time to time about organisation's goals, achievements and their responsibilities.

— Mastery of technical competencies can be done through regular exposure to new knowledge and skills. Each person should be encouraged to attend conferences, training, distance education and higher education courses for personal and professional growth.

— Training should help in strengthening instructional competencies of extension personnel.

Content Areas for Training

Extension personnel vary in position and nature of work from organisation to organisation. However, within the state departments there are three broad levels of extension personnel viz. field level or grass-root level village extension workers, middle level extension personnel such as subject-matter specialist and top level extension personnel such as extension managers (Mishra, 1990). The nature and level of contents would vary from one hierarchy to another. It is a general rule that as individual move above the ladders of hierarchy, they need less exposure of technical specialisation and more of management skills. In general, the job of extension worker, irrespective of position, involves a strange mix of roles as adult educator, technical specialist, programme executive and specialist in solving rural problems. Thus they require knowledge and skills in the field of technical specialisation, extension teaching, management, rural society and its problems, as elaborated below.

Technical Specialisation

Extension personnel by way of their pre-service education belong to one of the technical fields viz. Agriculture, Veterinary, Fisheries, Forestry, etc. Their involvement with particular works such as rice or pulse oilseed, dryland area or watershed management may sometimes make them more specialised. Thus, they may need training to upgrade knowledge and skills in this technical specialisation.

Extension Teaching Methods

Farmers as learners present unique challenges because of their socio-cultural background and lack of formal learning. On the other hand they have rich experiences in their vocation. Thus, extension personnel as adult educators must be acquainted with the principles of learning appropriate for adults. They should also know participative methods that can motivate learning. A range of methods and media of communications are available now. Thus, the training courses can be planned to acquaint extension personnel with principle and procedures of extension teaching as also preparation and use of communication media.

Management of Extension

Management refers to the process by which people, technology, job, task and other resources are combined and coordinated to achieve organisational objectives. Various function of management has been categorised under acronym POSDCORB (Planning, Organising, Staffing, Directing, Co-ordinating, Reporting and Budgeting). Management, however, involves much more than implementation of POSDCORB functions. Indeed, it requires an awareness of the organisation's goals. Extension personnel should become aware of their personnel attributes and learn to use them to work as a team to influence others to co-operate in achieving organisational goals. Thus, training in motivation, team-building, interpersonnel communication, etc. are essential.

Understanding Rural Society and its Problems

Every society has its own system of values, beliefs and institutions. People operate out of their own beliefs and values. Different groups have their power figures who matter in villages. Thus, extension work which aims at bringing change through introduction of innovation, is affected by a number of factors rooted in rural social environment. Language, festival, community relationships, sources of communication, class structure, prestige symbols, etc. vary from society to society. Thus, extension personnel need a conceptual framework to a analyse folk knowledge and practices and unravel psychological impediments to extension work at the grassroots. It is believed that marked changes are happening in rural social organisation and pattern of living. Leadership pattern is changing drastically. It is thus imperative that greater understanding of rural social dynamics be developed amongst extension personnel.

Types of Training

According to different stages in the career span of extension personnel, there are mainly three types of training viz. pre-service, induction and in-service training.

Pre-service Training

As the name indicates, this is a type of training conducted prior to entry in the job. Thus, this is a type of professional training which prepares a person for job. It includes university or college education after which a person is considered eligible for a job. There is direct link between the curriculum of pre-service training and nature of job to be performed.

Induction Training

This is a training given to entrant soon after appointment in order to familiarise him with the philosophy of organisation, procedure of day-to-day work and code of conduct. This is quite practical and related with particular job position. Good induction training is helpful reducing initial stress about performance and acquainting the incumbent with resources and skills required to perform effectively.

In-service Training

It includes all types of training during the service span of a person in the organisation. It is aimed to fill specific gaps at different points of time in career. This covers refresher training, overseas training, training for acquiring professional qualification etc. In-service training should ideally be practical-focussed, research-based and need-based.

Existing Training Opportunities for Extension Personnel

Training of extension personnel has received utmost attention ever since launching of the Community Development Programme in the country. Over the past four decades a strong infrastructure of training has been created to impart quality training in agriculture and allied technologies, extension methods, communication media, and extension management. With the introduction and expansion of training and visit extension system, training programmes for all levels of extension personnel have been streamlined as given below.

There is provision of regular training under the new system of extension supported by the World Bank. Monthly workshop and fortnightly training are two regular opportunities for training. Besides refresher training called as orientation workshop and other in-service trainings are also organised.

Monthly Workshop

Monthly workshop is organised for the Subject Matter Specialists (SMS) at State Agricultural University or its out-stations. The objective of this training is to provide skills which can meet the needs. The researcher also get to know the fields' problems. They discuss technical recommendations to be passed on the village-level functionaries for next one month. Monthly workshop is supposed to be exemplary and practical focussed so that SMSs can emulate techniques of training also. The Chief Scientists of respective subjects at the State Agricultural Universities Act as Master Trainers. Monthly workshop should have scope of visit to field and laboratory to acquaint SMSs about new technologies being tried. In brief, monthly workshop has been accorded a place of importance in the chain of training.

Fortnightly Training

Village Extension Workers (VEWs) and Agricultural Extension Officers (AEOs) are trained in fortnightly training held once in a fortnight. VEWs and AEOs share farmers reactions and learn recommendations for next fortnight SMSs and Training Officers helps in organising the training. This is an opportunity to learn technical skills and seek clarification regarding problems being faced in the field.

Orientation Training

Besides, the above two regular trainings, there is provision for orientation trainings once every year in order to orient extension personnel about various aspects of training and visit system.

Training of Trainers

As training is one of the vital components of training and visit system, provision has been made for training of various level of extension personnel in training methodologies so that effective training can be organised. The grassroot level extension functionaries are trained in Gramsewak Training Centres/Extension Training Centres and Farmers Training Centres. The trainers of these institutions as well as SMSs are trained at Extension Education Institutes in training methodology.

Training Institutions

At national level, Directorate of Extension, Ministry of Agriculture and Co-operation is involved in planning training courses in consultation with State Agricultural Universities, ICAR Institute, Central Institute, ICAR, State Departments of Agriculture and other concerned institutions. However, training of extension personnel is basically the responsibility of State Government. Most of the training requirements are met within the State in collaboration with State Agricultural Universities and other state level training institutions. Training in specialised subject-matter areas like communication extension management or technology management is co-ordinated by the Directorate of Extension, Government of India, and executed through specialised institutions. A network of training institution have come up in a country as given below :

— ICAR Institutes
— State Agricultural Universities (SAU)
— Advanced Centres of Training (ACT)
— National Centre for Management of Agricultural Extension (MANAGE)
— State level Training Institutes. viz. State Institute of Rural Development.
— Gramsewak Training of Centre /Extension Training Centre.

State Agricultural Universities

State Agricultural Universities have an important role in imparting training for extension personnel at the middle rung. They run national courses in agricultural technology or Extension and Communication methods in chosen areas with the help and support from Directorate of Extension, Government of India. SAUS have direct responsibilities to train the extension personnel from State Department of Agriculture. SAUS are the venues of monthly workshops meant for regular training of subject matter specialists under training and visit systems they may also organize suitable courses through State Department of Agriculture. Many SAUs have participants from other developing nations like Nepal, Sri Lanka, Nigeria, etc. for overseas training.

Advanced Centres of Training (ACTs)

Advanced Centres of Training (ACTs) have been created for improving specialised and quality training in chosen subject matter areas. They are located at SAUs, ICAR Institutes or Crop Research Directorate of ICAR. They are meant for training of senior and middle level extension personnel. They should be able to provide state of the art of technologies irrespective of subject matter areas but also balanced training delivery.

MANAGE

This is an apex level institution meant for training of senior Extension Managers. MANAGE has country-wide responsibility to upgrade quality training and enhance extension management. The focus of its training is on extension project planning and administration, extension personnel management, training of extension personnel, research extension linkages in extension projects and monitoring and evaluation of extension projects. Efforts have been made to create adequate infrastructure to provide quality training. Of late, it has undertaken past-graduate diploma programme in agri-business management.

Extension Education Institute

There are four Extension Education Institutes (EEI) in the country located at Anand (Gujarat), Nilokheri (Haryana), Hyderabad (Andhra Pradesh) and Jorhat (Assam) and meant for training of middle extension personnel extension education concepts, extension methods, communication media and training methodology. They are attatched with State Agricultural Universities. EEIs are also involved in teaching of extension education leading to M.Sc. and Ph.D. degrees. Besides, they also publish supporting materials and provide consultancy.

Extension Training Centres/Gramsewak Training Centre

Extension Training Centres (ETCs) and Gramsewak Training Centres (GTCs) are meant to provide induction of in-service training to grassroot level village functionaries i.e. village level extension worker. They had been established during the Community Development Programme.

REFERENCES

Haiman, F.S. (1950). *Group Leadership and Democratic Action,* Houghton Miffin Company, New York.

Hansra, B.S. and Kumar, B. (1997). *Training Methodology for Human Resource Development,* Classical Publishing Co., New Delhi.

Iffner, P.L. and A.F. Douds (1988). *Train the Trainer — Practical Skills that Work,* HRD Press, Massachusetts, U.S.A.

I.L.O. (1986). *Vocational Training, Glossry of Selected Terms of International Labour Office,* Geneva.

Lynton, R.P. and Pareek, U. (1967). *Training for Development.* Illinois, Richard D. Irwin, Inc.

Reddy, S.V. and Sahay, B.N. (1973). Differential characteristics of farm leaders in a progressive and non-progressive village, *Indian Journal of Extension Education,* 9(3&4), pp. 87-91.

Strayton, R. (1986). Organisation of courses and conferences in ILO, Chapter 21, International Labour Organisation, Geneva.

Tead, O. (1951). *The Art of Administration,* McGraw Hill, New York.

5

TRANSFER OF TECHNOLOGY IN AGRICULTURE

OVERVIEW

There is increasing use of the term Transfer of Technology (TOT) by extension practitioners now-a-days. Can technologies be transferred mechanically in linear fashion? Do the terms 'extension' and 'TOT' mean one and the same thing? TOT includes more than mere dissemination of information. There are many conceptual models of TOT emphasizing on different elements of the process. Extension can play crucial role in preventing imbalances caused due to input-intensive of new agricultural technology among resource poor farmers. In fact, extension can create awareness and equip both farmers and scientists to work together to generate technologies appropriate to the local situation. It requires new methods and perspectives to work in close touch with people. It is in this context that new concepts like Farming Systems Research and Extension, Participatory Technology Development, Participatory Rural Appraisal, Rapid Rural Appraisal, Indigenous Technological Knowledge, etc. are becoming more meaningful.

WHAT DOES THE TERM TECHNOLOGY MEAN ?

Technology means application of science to the practical aim of human life. It refers to the transformation of scientific laws into machines, tools, mechanical devices, instruments, innovations, procedure and techniques to attain tangible ends or manipulate environment for practical purposes. Technology has been taken from Greek language. 'Techno' means art of doing or systematic way of working whereas 'logus' means knowledge or study. So technology is used for all those procedures or systematic ways of working by application of scientific law. Technology refers to both the hardware viz. machines, equipment and software such as programmes or procedure of working or running machines. Agricultural technologies refers to various techniques of crop production, crop improvement, crop protection, crop processing etc. e.g. multiple cropping, insects, tractors, integrated pest management.

Classification of Technologies

It is fashionable today to talk of modern or scientific technology. Many people ignorantly believe that all technologies are helpful. Conversely, it is also assumed that all traditional technologies are useless. None of them is absolutely true. Technologies are categorised into high, appropriate or intermediate groups.

High technologies are those capital and energy intensive technologies designed in developed nations to reduce labour and cater to market. In general, high technologies have some common features as below :

— They require heavy use of non-renewable resources.
— They generate large volume of toxic wastes.
— They depend on large, centralised, hierarchical organisations that require large capital investments and create dependency of users on suppliers.
— They create work opportunities for highly trained work forces.

Appropriate technology means a low-cost technology using mainly local or easily available materials and skills to meet a recognised need.

Intermediate technology. Many people consider appropriate technology as traditional or old, and primitive. In order to avoid such labels, the term intermediate technology was coined to refer to such small scale technologies emerging out of a gradual process of technological innovations sustainable in the communities. It avoids pitfalls of high technologies especially exploitation of natural and human resources. Such technologies are more natural, non-polluting and can be locally owned and produced in small units. They have respect for ecology, food, energy, shelter and water need of the communities.

Transfer of Technology (TOT)

Transfer in common parlance means change of place or physical movement or mechnical transport. Does the phrase 'transfer of technology' mean merely taking a new idea or procedure or product from extension or research institution to farmers' field. Even if we take TOT literally, no idea or product can be moved just by lifting it physically. Mere physical shift will not ensure its use. People are not passive recipient to apply a technology just because it was brought or told. Thus, this transfer of information cannot lead to acceptance. People have their attitudes, opinions, values and established ways of doing things. New technology has to compete and work within the context and environment of people. Extent of acceptance is influenced by a variety of personal as well social, environmental and resource factors. Acceptance demands new learning and adjustment.

Thus, TOT is not push button shifting of technology. People are rational. They adopt new technology if they are convinced about its utility. The technology must be compatible with social and cultural systems. In view of the discussions about technologies and their acceptance in social systems, it can be concluded that TOT refers to the entire process of technology development, processing, dissemination and integration through research, extension and farming systems (in case of agriculture) keeping in view the resources, organisational limitations and capabilities of the three systems to solve the problem of society. This means that TOT is not a linear process with distinct parts and roles of research, extension and farming system. It is a collaborative effort between the three partners. Each of the three functions of technology development, processing and dissemination has to be done in consultation with each other.

- Let it be concluded that TOT refers to the activities of research systems (State Agricultural Universities, Indian Council of Agricultural Research, Agricultural College, Private research organisations, etc., extension system and farmers' system.
- In order to be accepted and integrated into social systems, technologies must be developed keeping in view farmers' existing practices, resources, environment and preferences.
- Technologies must provide solution to farmers' problems.
- Communication of technologies alone is not enough. The other aspect viz. infrastructure, support services policy, marketing, input,

training, etc. must be assured for effective utilisation.

TOT IN AGRICULTURE

Conventional agricultural research and technology transfer efforts were more concerned with increasing production. The researches were conducted on large farms with the help of heavy doses of external inputs. Technique of genetics and plant breeding were employed to enhance the productivity. These high yielding strains required heavy doses of chemicals for soil and plant nutrition as well protection. Assured irrigation was critical for their success. As a result, the new high yielding varieties of rice and wheat increased production manifolds. They stimulated development of irrigation and other infrastructure for providing much needed supply of inputs for new cultivation. As a result, the benefits of these technologies were more evident among larger farmers and more developed regions. Resource poor subsistence farmers and risk-prone (flood affected, dryland etc.) areas were least affected. There were several other undesirable social consequences like class-conflict and mass migration of labour force in economically developed belts. Extreme dependency of farms on external sources for inputs also added to their owes. New agricultural technologies have several distinguishing features as below.

— They are input intensive and expensive.
— They are market oriented rather than consumption based.
— They require complex technical knowledge and skills.
— They require network of institutional arrangement.
— They are more vulnerable to insects/pests and diseases.

New agricultural technologies bring many ecological problems such as salinity, soil erosion, surface as also ground water pollution, etc. The undesirable effects of new agricultural technology on natural resources have raised the issue of sustainability. Whether agriculture in its present form has capacity to remain productive while maintaining the resource base? According to TAC/CGIAR 1988 'sustainable agriculture is the successful management of resources for agriculture to satisfy changing human needs while maintaining or enhancing the quality of the environment and conserving natural resources'. Thus, sustainability of agriculture calls for conservation and enhancement of ecology, economy and social change along with increase in production.

MODELS OF TOT

Historically, transfer of technologies have occurred as a result of cultural contact and migration. Transfer of industrial technologies across nations have been the result of bilateral treaties between industrialized nation and the developing ones. However, transfer of agricultural technologies have been seen as the process of research extension and farmers organisation. The roles of each organisation, extent of initiative and interactions between each organisation and tools and techniques of working have varied from time to time and place to place in view of the philosophical orientation about technologies and development. There are three major trends in the way TOT is carried out. The oldest and most common approach is known by many names top-down modulor converntional model. Next, there is some modification over the conventional one to consider farmers reaction, known as feedback model. The third and recent approach is known as participatory model. There are several other models supporting one or the other tenets as discussed below.

Conventional Model

This is the most prevalent model so far, ever since the beginning of agricultural research and extension. Technological innovations generated in the light of basic science researches, in the wake of industrialization, provided the basis for quantum leap in agricultural production. Thus, need for extending such technologies to farmers was felt so that farmers are motivated to adopt and diffuse. Some of the important features of this model are given below :

— Technology generation was the sole responsibility of the researchers. Interaction with farmers or extension personnel was not seen as relevant.
— Farmers were seen as passive recipient of technologies.
— There was little or no contact between farmers and scientists.
— Role of extension was to persuade farmers to adopt new technologies.

Thus, this model suffered from feelings of superiority about scientists and technologies. Users' problems and views were not given consideration due for solving their problems. Such an approach was evident in green revolution.

Feedback Model

Disenchantment with green revolution agriculture based on excessive use of external inputs such as new crop varieties, inputs, irrigation, machines etc. called for new approach of TOT. Many International Agricultural Research Centres were interested in evolving a farmers' orientation in agricultural research. Thus, feedback model emerged with the following salient features.

- Identification of target group, his problems and reaction is valued by researches.
- There is close interaction between research and extension systems as evident in Farming Systems Research and Extension and Training and visit extension systems.
- Researches are carried out both on research farms as well as farmers' field to take into account resource and other variables at farmers' sites.
- Team of researchers included extension personal as well as social scientists to have holistic understanding of the farmers' problems. Interrelatedness of various factors of farm and home were taken into account.

However, feedback model was still based on the initiatives of the scientists and farmers were consulted. The initiative, inquisitiveness and wisdom of farmers were still not utilized. It was thought by many humanistically oriented researches that there is need to unleash the creativity and initiative of farmers as well.

Farmers Participatory Models

There is recent need trend to strengthen farmers' capacities for research and extension for enhancing sustainable development in rural areas. The new model is based on several observations about the research and extension initiatives in many areas of the world. By virtue of keen interest, strong affiliation with vocation and experience, farmers have inherent interest in experimentation with new way of farming. Their indigenous wisdom and understanding of agroecological conditions are great resources for evolving appropriate technologies. Thus, new model had taken a stand that researches must begin and end with farmers. The key characteristics of such approach are as given below:

— Farmers are seen as active partner in research and extension.
— Indigenous wisdom possessed by farmers are valued and considered.
— Research is seen a joint endeavour involving farmers and researchers to solve problems being faced by farmers.
— Establishment of physical infrastructure and educational facilities for strengthening local experimentation is an essential aspect of participatory model.
— It emphasises on the need for scientists to become more sensitive to understand, communicate and collaborate with farmers.

Thus the new model of TOT is farmer-oriented and non-perspective. It does not underrate the value of either scientific agricultural researches carried out by the academic institutions nor does it ignore the farmers initiatives. In fact, emphasis is on encouraging farmers groups to organise themselves and network together for strengthening process of technology development. It is complementary, farmer-focussed and self-reliant. It sees the significance of indigenous channels of communication existing in rural areas in farmer to farmer extension. Thus, a new role of scientists, extension personnel, farmers and others is clearly evident in this model. As a result of the recent development in TOT approaches, classical image of researches as academicians in the secure environments of universities, colleges or research institution is no more valid. Agricultural researchers to be able to generate appropriate technologies must have sensitivity to the limitation of farmers and extension worker. They should be ready to live, work and learn from both farmers and extension worker. They should respect the knowledge available at the other side of the fence. Problem-solving, must necessarily begin with initiatives at the farmers' level. Thus extension has a new role to play.

Other Models

Besides these three mega trends in TOT approach, there are many other conceptual models highlighting different aspects of the TOT process, as elaborated below.

Technology Innovation Process

Technology innovation process (TIP) has been considered as chronological sequence of events from research, development, testing, adoption, integration, diffusion to common practice. According to this model, distinction between research and extension, as advocated in several models is not real. Extension to be able to play the linking roles must start at technology generation stage. Futther, the role of research as generator of knowledge must also consider knowledge related to social system. Thus, knowledge about linking systems is part of the research process. In fact, each of the functions under TIP are interrelated and need to be put under same administrative framework. Social Sciences knowledge is of immense value in designing technologies understanding about farmers needs, interests, problems and capacity of organisation to generate technologies and deliver through linkage can be a lot helpful, technology innovation process is a social process with capacity to develop human resource through integrated functioning (McDermott, 1988).

MIDDA Model

Model for Innovation Development Diffusion and Adoption (MIDDA) provides theoretical perspective representing general problems and potentials inherent in three sub-system of TOT viz. research and development, diffusion and farming sub-systems. All the three sub-systems operate under society and other external forces. Various exogenous variables viz. government policy, incentive system, regulation, market place, cost-sharing device between production and conservation affect the process. The specific functions and assumption of three systems are as given below :

Research and Development Sub-system

Researches conducted by various government, commercial/private and voluntary organisations as well as farmers inventions are also considered as part of the sub-system. There is need for both experimental (controlled) research and farm level experimentation to generate appropriate solutions. The whole farm including crop production, animal production, agro-chemical, machines, water use etc. are considered for diagnosing interrelatedness of problems. Linkages are required between various research organisations as well.

Diffusion Sub-system

MIDDA assumes that responsibility for diffusion of innovation to communities lies with institution. The extension messages coming from government, commercial organisation, voluntary organisation, and farm communities should be taken into account to make it more comprehensive. Institutional structure, methods, personnel and training of each of these organisations need to be examined by social scientists including social psychologists, extension educationists and management specialists.

Farming Community Sub-system

In past, innovativeness had been considered from view point of technology. Thus Farming Systems Research considered different categories of farmers according to socio-economic status, access to resource, agro-climatic conditions, etc. However, MIDDA considers the need to assess food consumption and production, conservations of environment and their relations on farming in order to generate relevant technologies. Formal linkage between diffusion sub-system and farming community need to be institutionalised. Linkage is needed between farm level experimentations and research stations. An array of existing channels of communication available with farmers need to be explored. Besides, social scientists need to diagnose problems of farm communities as well as organisations in order to deliver messages effectively.

Farmer-back-to-Farmer Model (Rhoades and Booth, 1982)

This is a problem-solving model which assumes that research should begin with those who have the problems. Farmers are considered active members of joint diagnostic team to search problems. Farmers with their long association and experience with local agro-ecological, social and organisational system are better equipped to provide relevant experience. The four main activities in the model includes diagnosis of problems by technologist and social scientists as well as farmer, inter-disciplinary research, adapting/testing on-farm/research station and farmer evaluation and adaptation.

Havlock's Technology Generation, Adaptation and Utilization Model

This model assumes that pure or basic research provide knowledge base for applied research and generation technologies. Project managers should know how to adapt technologies on the basis of feedback from users. The sub-systems in the model include pure or basic research, applied research, practitioner's adaptation and user or intended beneficiary. One of the most common problems throughout the developing world is lack of communication and co-ordination between research organisation and extension services. Thus, extension services are to be managed to make relevant technologies available and adaptable in useable form by field worker and intended beneficiaries.

ROLE OF EXTENSION IN TRANSFER OF TECHNOLOGY

'Extension' and 'Transfer of Technology' are not synonymous as many people may assume. Extension refers to the educational process in solving problems of farmers or ruralites in agriculture. Thus, it necessarily has a teaching function (Mishra 1990). TOT includes additional function of input supply and agro-services. Extension also helps in developing organisation and leadership. TOT is much wider term and includes process of technology development, adaptation, dissemination and integration into farmers' system. While TOT, when appropriate, is part of any extension services responsibility. TOT should not be concerned with only mechanically disseminating technologies to the rural clientele. It should rather take into account the other accompaniments and pre-conditions necessary for integration of technologies into the social system.

Adoption of new technologies requires learning and decision making. Such decisions are influenced by a number of factors other than technology. Farmers, knowledge, skills, values, personal resources, environmental as well as socio-cultural backgrounds affect their decisions. A new technology may demand replacement and many adjustments. TOT, thus, requires effective co-ordination between various organisations as well. It has been realized by experts that development of technology in isolation from users creates more problems. Agricultural technologies generated at well-endowed research farms are input intensive and expensive. They require network of institutional arrangements to assure access to credits, inputs, advice, market, irrigation, electricity etc. These factors form a mix in that they must all be there, in addition to access to technology and knowledge (Rolling, 1922). The undesirable consequences of agricultural technologies in terms of environmental pollution, ecological imbalance and degradation of natural resources have been highlighted by several observers. Thus, extension cannot be passive communicator of technology rather it has to play other roles as well so as to make innovation development and extension more participatory. Some of the important roles of extension, as explained by several experts, (Chambers, 1991; Rolling, 1992 and Walker, 1994) have been elaborated below.

Extension should help in strengthening Farmers' Involvement in Technology Development

It is now increasingly realized that farmers are not only consumers of technology but they also have creativity and local knowledge required to contribute to development of technologies. In the process of developing technologies appropriate to the socio-cultural systems, knowledge of local resources, farming system, agroecological condition, etc. of the area are invaluable help. Farmers by virtue of their association with farming as traditional vocation, possess accumulated wisdom of the community. Such wisdom is not available to people external to the social system.

Extension should help in Development of Rural People's Organisation

The problem of rural areas cannot be solved by the efforts of the government alone. The poor and the marginalised farmers have often remained away from the benefits planned for them through various programmes. Thus, the large number of such oppressed groups have to be strengthened by organising on the basis of homogeneity in problems and other socio-cultural factors. Help should not be provided through extension organisations to develop their leadership. Such grassroot organisations can become strong fora for articulating people's need and involving people in technology development and extension. That is why many countries have started experimenting with what is called as participatory Technology Development (PTD) through people's organisation. PTD, to be successful in the long run, require permanent organisational structures. If extension is to play a role in long term agricultural development, much more attention must be given to developing local leadership and farmers, organisation. A programme which depends on simple dissemination of information to farmers and neglects developing local initiative through groups action will not make a lasting contribution. Developing local organisations with links to extension and training of local leaders is important if the objective is to create initiative and confidence (Lowder Milk, 1982).

Extension can help in Conscientization

Paulo Freiri's concept of conscientization as a tool of development has lot of relevance in the context of developing nations for the small and marginal farmers. Deep roots of traditions and several physical and psychological constraints obstruct participation of the poor. In the words of Paulo Freiri, a culture of silence prevails. There is need to help people to critically analyse their situations, problems and capacities. Such objective thinking alone can make people conscious. A certain level of awareness and confidence is essential pre-condition for development. Thus, extension should not be involved in just passing technology. Rather, it should facilitate a process of dialogue. No doubt, such efforts require a cadre of conscientized extension workers as well.

Extension should play Supportive Role with other Agencies

It is a common knowledge that extension agency has a major role in providing technologies appropriate to the needs of target group. However, by virtue of its proximity with rural clientele, it is in a better position to perform linking role with research and other supporting agencies viz. credit, inputs, irrigation, etc. Extension cannot be effective in the absence of critical inputs and services. World Bank Officials identified (a) appropriate technology, (b) attractive markets, and (c) available inputs as the critical ingredients for successful development. Extension's effectiveness will be dependent on those ingredients, which are outside its direct control (Russel).

Extension should be closely linked with Research Right from the beginning

Conventional models of technology generation and transfer assumed research and extension as segregated organisations with distinct set of roles. The role of extension, in fact, started after the research had produced innovations. However, in order to generate user focussed technologies appropriate to agro-ecological as well resource characteristics of farmers, it is essential that extension workers actively participate in identifying problems. It should also help in equipping rural clientele and ascertaining their preferences. Extension because of its close links with farmers and rural communities, can better help in focussing attention of researchers on real problems. A holistic view of the farmers' situation can be helpful.

TOT approach has failed to deliver goods because research organisations have worked in complete isolation from the target population, within narrow confines of academic specializations. As a result, realities of rural clientele in diverse agro-ecological and socio-economic conditions have not been given due considerations in development of technology. In recent years, TOT paradigm has been criticised and questioned. Non-adoption of high input-intensive technologies cannot be attributed to ignorance of farmers any more. Thus there is shift in understanding about approaches of technology development and dissemination which are more decentralised, people centred, self-reliant and sustainable. Extension as a strong arm of the government cannot remain neutral. A conscientised extension organisation with emphasis on developing people's organisations, Leadership, capacity to experiment as well as involve in technology development is required today. No doubt, this call for national policy and reorganisation.

EMERGING CONCEPTS IN TRANSFER OF TECHNOLOGY

Development of new technologies and their integration into farmers' social systems are of paramount importance to developing nations with predominantly agricultural economy. New viewpoints are regularly coming up to mitigate the imbalances caused by new technologies to large majority of small farms. Thus the emphases of agricultural research and extension are shifting. The segregation of research and extension organisations from farmers is being questioned. There is increasing concern on holistic understanding of farmers' farming as well as socio-political environment to be able to unravel several connections of technology. Such understanding demands close proximity and participatory methods of working together. Thus, many new concepts and approaches are emerging to give new direction to TOT. The first departure from conventional discipline-based research, has been noticed in farming systems research and extension. Participatory Technology Development (PTD) is a new strategy for development of intervention that fully acknowledges the superiority of rurals people's accumulated wisdom and benefits of scientists. The strategy emphasises on community-based organisations to strengthen people's capabilities for technology development and extension. Besides, such approaches calls for new methods of working with people. Rapid Rural Appraisal (RRA), Participatory Rural Appraisal (RRA), Indigenous Technological Knowledge (ITK), Networking, etc. are increasingly being talked about now to support the new approaches. An attempt has been made here to discuss such emerging concepts.

Farming Systems Research/Extension (FSR/E)

Rationale for FSR/E

FSR/E evolved in 1970s as an alternative to conventional research and extension which had propagated technologies requiring high external inputs. The standard role of extension was to disseminate package of practices. Such technologies were not beneficial for resource poor farmers in risk-prone areas. As a result, several undesirable consequences were observed in many parts of the country. Rural strife, migration of labour force to industrial areas and pauperisation of marginal farmers were observed in many Asian countries. Thus, an alternative approach to generation and dissemination of technology was tried at several International Agricultural Research Centres (IARC) with a view to make farmers as collaborator than passive recipient and generate technologies that solves their problems. Such approach also supports integration of research and extension.

Characteristics of FSR/E

FSR/E is farmer-based, problem solving, comprehensive, interdisciplinary, complementary, iterative, dynamic and responsible to the society (Shaner *et al.*, 1982).

Farmer-based

FSR/E shows its interest in farmers' situation and perception through its close contact using observation, discussion, trial etc. Farmers' reactions are taken into account at every step.

Problem-solving

FSR/E categorises farmers on homogeneous characteristic and investigates problems. Emphasis is placed on priority aspects with conditions of farmers in view.

Comprehensive

FSR/E does not work piece meal on specialized areas as agronomy, plant protection or processing but takes total setting in which farms operate into consideration.

Interdisciplinary

Farmer has to perform many functions of farm and home. Thus, the team of researchers offering solution also comprise of various related disciplines including sociology and economics to understand interrelation of complex farming problems.

Complementary
FSR/E builds on research, production and extension work of many others.

Iterative
It facilitates continuous learning and changes because of the interaction and quick work.

Dynamic
FSR/E is not single, well-planned, carefully thought out master plan but a gradual process that continually re-evaluates research results and farmers' conditions.

Responsible to Society
FSR/E considers not only farming problems but also the broader interests of the society as well.

Activities
FSR involves a set of activities beginning from target and research area selection to problem diagnosis and development of relevant agenda, planning and design of on-farm research and extension of research results. A basic elements of the scheme constant collaborations and rapport among researchers, extension personnel and farmers extension personnel have important role to play at each of the steps of FSR/E.

Five basic activities of FSR/E (Shaner *et al.*, 1982)

Step 1. Locating target area, stratifying into sub-areas, according to critical physical biological and socio-economic factors to get reasonable degree of homogeneity in conditions to ensure applicability of technologies. Research site is selected keeping effectiveness of site for conducting research in view. The extension agents can pass the knowledge of local conditions in this regard.

2. Interdisciplinary research team scouts new areas, reviews secondary data and conduts quick reconnaissance surveys, on-farm

experiment as well as formal survey to identify problems and opportunity by improving. They build their knowledge of the research area .

3. This sets stage for on-farm research programmes. Research teams review problems and opportunities, identified from the earlier activity, apprise their organization's capacity, consider applicability of available technologies, make assumptions above near-term condition, sets research priorities. Extension staff can contribute a lot here in terms of knowledge about local environment.

4. *On-farm research and analysis*
   Three types of on-farm researches are conducted viz. research managed trials, superimposed trials and farmer managed tests. The first is similar to research conducted on experiment stations, except that it is conducted on farmers' fields with the intent of learning how technologies are suited to farmers' condition. The second, when researchers identify condition in farmers' fields that ripe for improvement; and third experiment managed by farmers in a way FSR team learns how farmers react to proposed changes. Farmers' modification to the experiment are as important as experiment's results.
   Monitoring of on-farm research to keep track of biological results as well as learning from productive activities. Records of farmer follow-up survey of household and farmers production practices on experiments research under controlled conditions.
   Extension staff assist in monitoring and involving farmers in the process.

5. *Extension of results*
   It refers to further investigation of technologies before transfer. How it can fare well in broad and more intensive scale. Multi-location testings are required.

Participatory Technology Development (PTD)

Rationale

Keeping in view the limitations of new agricultural technologies to solve the production problems of a large majority of small farmers, there has been frantic search for alternative approach to develop useful technologies. There is a call to make farmers more active partner in technology development process. PTD is a process of bringing together the local communities with their own knowledge and capacity for research, on one platform with the researchers and other professionals. PTD process is aimed at strengthening existing experimental capacity of farmers in search of sustainable innovation generation system.

Farmers like anyone else are curious lot and keep trying new ideas. There are many cases of successful solutions offered by the farmers to agricultural problems in past. However, in practice this trait of farmers is never encouraged. PTD helps in systematising farm-based spontaneous research by real people who are experienced about the area and cultivation practices. Moreover, they have a stake in this research. In promoting farmers as experimenters many obstacles emerge due to traditional attitudes and training of professionals. Professionals with agricultural expertise need to acquire social skills and exposure to anthropological and social tools. It requires respect for Indigenous Technological Knowledge (ITK) embedded in local society. ITK is rooted in concrete reality of day-to-day living. This also gives farmers equal status as expert. ITK is distributed among various economic groups, age and gender. There ITK may have potential for development through research. PTD has been tried extensively through Institute of Development Studies (IDS), Sussex, UK. Five categories of activities have been reported (Havecort *et al.*, 1991) in most documents dealing with PTD.

1. *How to get started ?*

This requires one to build rapport with farmers and other partners in research process. Encouragement is needed to build trust and discuss problems and situation. The idea is to build common platform for understanding the conditions and locate problem to work on.

2. *Looking for things to try*

Identification of indigenous technical knowledge and formal knowledge screening and selecting topics, using criterion leading to optimal use of local resources need to be explored.

3. Trying out developing joint capacity for experimentation, plan and implement results and evaluation.

4. *Sharing results*
Communication of results with other local and scientific networks to scrutinize and interpret them and incite others to adopt and test.

5. *Sustaining and consolidating system of PTD*
Creating favourable conditions for farmers' organisations, local institutions and support at policy level. Establishing physical infrastructure and other facilities for local experiment and management of research.

These steps are only suggestive and not rigid. PTD is still evolving organisational development, training and other institutional issues.

Rapid Rural Appraisal (RRA)

Rationale
Planning for rural development requires authentic information to provide right solution. Experiences of development in past showed that experts need better method to collect accurate and relevant information. Short visits to rural areas or lengthy surveys often do not provide the realistic picture of the situation. In order to meet such needs, RRA evolved as cost-effective and appropriate approach. Thus, RRAs came to be handy tool for collecting local insight and quality information needed for experts from outside to plan solutions to rural problems. These methods valued traditional knowledge and wisdom of people which local people possess naturally as they belong to the culture outsiders can easily obtain these through RRA.

What is RRA?
RRA is a way of collecting and analyzing information from field in short period of time. RRA uses multiple methods and involves people to collect and validate information and does not rest on anyone method.

Special features

1. Use of RRA demands respect for ITK.
Local people operate in the existing situation by virtue of their understanding of the environment. They have their own reasons and approach to cope with the situation. Experts must feel respect for basic knowledge that people possess.

2. Experts must learn from people in terms of their (people's) perception of things. One has to become a learner and appreciate the criteria and categories of the people in describing things. This requires forgetting much of the technical jargons and advanced techniques.

3. It allows for natural learning which can take place through observation and interaction. It is informal flexible and creative way of gradual learning.
4. It requires experts to come in direct contact with people and area.
5. It allows one to try different methods in order to get closer to truth.

Different RRA Methods

Using existing information

There is a wealth of information already existing in every area in the form of reports, books, student researches, and government records. Local newspapers and magazines are also rich sources to look for.

Learning Local Knowledge

Rural people know their soil, weather, plants, cultural practices and ways to live in difficult situation. This may be explored to understand the rationale validity and values.

Direct Observation

There is no substitute to observation as far as verification of information is concerned. One can always take time to see and check how things operate. This may validate the data collected from other sources.

Key Information

There are always people in every society who possess a wealth of information by virtue of their occupation, interest or experience. They also have a tendency to interact and share such information. It is better to get more accurate information from these people than those who may live but are not well acquainted themselves. It takes time to locate such people and open up with them. It requires to check with other people as well.

Group Interview

It is a common knowledge that group has a power to legitimise. Thus, people open up and talk more forcefully of ideas supported in group.

Many local information are hard to get individually. People feel less threatened when in group.

Rapid rural appraisal look to be common-sensical and many experts do not consider it worthwhile to use. However, they are more human and natural way to gain insights about local area.

Participatory Rural Appraisal (PRA)

Rationale

Participatory Rural Appraisal (PRA) grew out of a general feeling of users of PRA that farmers/ruralites are being extracted for information. Farmers do not truly learn or participate. The question then was of evolving quick methods of collecting field data which at the same time benefit people to learn about their problem, analyse and gain consciousness. Hence, certain elements were required to make PRA more participatory and empowering.

What is PRA ?

PRA is a methodology for interacting with villagers and seeking their participation in putting forward their points of views about problems, analyse them, and use the learning. PRA takes into account people's indigenous knowledge. It is learning through participation about livelihood system and interaction of various facts. It helps in joint evaluation of problems and opportunities.

Features of PRA

1. 'PRA' is concerned with collecting information through participation.
2. It helps farmers to put forth their perception in their own language and modes of communication. Thus, use of symbols, maps and drawings are made not in standard forms of art but as villagers can do naturally.
3. It requires living and looking at life from close quarters using methods that enable participation and learning. It emphasises on listening to people's experiences, history, culture, priorities and performances.
4. It encourages multi-disciplinary investigation using multiple methods for cross-checking to allow different perspectives.
5. Attitude of listening, learning and respect for rural people is a must to conduct PRA so that mutual learning can take place.

PRA Methods

Diagramming : Diagramming helps in easy communication between researcher and villager. They help in cross-checking of information. They generate interests and more detailed discussion. Use of villager's own symbols and method of drawing gives them confidence and co-equal status to share their perceptions. This helps in building rapport. Diagrams encourage groups to critically discuss and give their own opinions. However, diagram may get too complex, sometimes, to explain.

Transact walk : Participatory transact walk is a group activity of villages and researches to walk along various agro-ecological zones of the village and discuss about land-use pattern, problems and rural ecological conditions. The experience of the participating villagers about their perceptions are discussed by the group. This would be quite revealing perception of people about natural resources of the village.

Ranking and Scoring : These methods provide chance to rural people to express their preferences and give reasons for liking certain items Here preference ranking, pairwise ranking, wealth ranking and relationship between two factors are explored. It involves preparation of list of households and assigning number to each. Then key informants are asked to rank individually according to their own criteria. The criteria used by them are discussed later. Final wealth classification are prepared on this basis.

Do it yourself : The activities of rural people can be understood better if experts also get opportunities to practise them and realise. It gives real ideas and help in getting along. People appreciate such gestures of physical help.

Maps and Models : Participatory mapping again releases creativity of people and reveal their ways of using symbols. People open up with enthusiasm using local materials. Discussion becomes easier.

Indigenous Technological Knowledge (ITK)

Every society has stock of knowledge generated within socio-cultural system in order to solve problems unique to it. Such indigenous knowledge are not only economic but also locally feasible. Undesirable consequences of new and exogenous technologies have drawn attention of experts to indigenous technological knowledge (ITK). However, wide variety of ITK is highly localised and restricted for outsiders because of indigenous overtones. It is passed on from one generation to another through word of mouth. Such knowledge is product of trial and error, natural selection and keen observations through centuries. (Chitirai Chelvan and Ramah, 1991). Many of the traditional knowledge in agriculture are always targetted for productivity, sustainability, stability and equality. Inventory of farm operations having association with Indigenous Knowledge (IK) or TK (Traditional Knowledge) includes cutting and burning, following, adjusting density or depth or time of planting, flooding, planting without tillage, multiple cropping, crop rotations, biological control of crop, pests, etc. (Dasgupta, 1993). It is essential to document and analyse ITK for the following reasons :

— Solutions to problem specific to various agro-ecological condition can be recorded, analysed and communicated.
— People in general are losing interest in ITK as outdated knowledge and hence it is necessary that precious knowledge is preserved.
— Sharing the accumulated knowledge with the farmers back will restore their pride in their innovative potential (Gupta 1990).
— Scientific investigation of ITK will provide it validity and encouragement.
— Farmer-to-farmer communication and learning would become feasible if ITK of one region is shared in the other region.

According to Gupta, Singh and Dubey (1994), traditional agricultural knowledge have the following characteristics.

— It has minimum risk factor
— It relies heavily on genetic and physical diversity.
— It exploits optimum utility of local resources
— It is environmentally healthy
— It takes a holistic world view
— It is readily available and easily understandable
— It is labour intensive
— It fits into local farming system and is adaptable to meet multipurpose needs
— It is based on cultural values of community
— It is attested by evidences from trustworthy, sources

It is thus essential to document traditional agricultural knowledge to understand their rationale and increase awareness among general masses. However, it is not easy to document them by outsiders. Thus, descriptive and narrative methods as used in Anthropology are more appropriate.

REFERENCES

Chamla, S. & Coughenour, M.C. (1987). Model for Innovation Development, Deffusion and Adoption (MIDDA) — A System for Agricultural Development, *Journal of Extension Systems,* 3(1), pp. 47-55.

Chambers, R. (1991). To make the flip strategies for working with undervalued resource agriculture, Participatory Technology Development in Sustainable Agriculture in *ILIEA,* 1991.

Havercort, B.; Hiemstra, W., Reijhtjes, C. and Essers, S. (1991). Strengthening Farmers' Capacity for Technology Development. *ILIEA,* 4(3), 1999.

Havelock, R.G. (1993). Planning for Innovation through Dissemination and Utilization of Knowledge, Univ. of Michigan, Ann Artour.

Lowdermilk, M.K. (1985). A System Process for Improving the Quality of Agricultural Extension, *Journal of Extension System,* 1:4J-J3, December.

Mukherjee, N. (1993). *Participatory Rural Appraisal, Methodology and Applications,* Concept Publishing Company, New Delhi.

Rolling, N. (1992). Applied Agricultural Research and Extension : Issue for Knowledge Management — *Journal of Extension Systems,* Vol. 8, pp. 167-170.

Walker, M. (1994). Agricultural Information System, Synergy and Development, *Journal of Extension Systems,* 10(2), pp. 1-15.

6

PHILOSOPHICAL BASIS FOR EXTENSION WORK

OVERVIEW

PHILOSOPHY literally means love for wisdom. Philosophy refers to the investigations about life and its various components. It is, in fact, an integrated view on the right conduct or 'What ought to be'. Thus, a man's view of 'What is right to do' indicates the kind of person he is. Such views serve as motivation for action. They reflect foundations of man's activities and the laws that govern them. Why is it essential to know philosophy of extension? Since, philosophy is a system of values and beliefs, knowledge of philosophy may guide one's work. It can become a tool for improving practice and consistent work-behaviour. There would not be confusion or conflict about the ultimate aim and approach of work. In any profession, one's conduct is sum of personal values, experiences and life style. Thus, philosophy is practical tool to provide rationale for decisions. The principles on the other hand are thumb rules for action. There are various approaches of extension work. The manner in which extension work has been executed around the world, has attracted criticism from scholars and onlookers. There is need to devise participatory approaches of extension work keeping the pious goals in view.

WHAT IS PHILOSOPHY ?

Philosophy owes its origin to the Greek words *'Phileo'* meaning love and 'Sophia' meaning wisdom. Thus, it literally means love for wisdom. In the early phases of its growth, philosophy embraced all branches of knowledge. Later with growth of sciences, range of subject matter dealt by it narrowed. However, philosophy concerns itself with the fundamental questions about human existence and its place in the world. The purpose of human life, its guiding values, forces of transformation, the way of knowing reality and deciding what is right, etc. are the concerns of philosophy. It is a special system of knowledge dealing with complex problems and question of life. The methods of inquiry in this case are indepth, logical, rigorous and holistic. Thus, philosophy is a system of knowledge with its own methods of inquiry to delve deep into the questions of human existence and laws in an integrated fashion.

Why Study Philosophy?

Often people perceive philosophy as something abstract or vague. It is commonly held that philosophy is the preserve of learned people or philosophers. This is not true. If philosophy is integrated view of life, every person needs values to decide what is right. Philosophy is interwoven in daily life. Those who believe in eat-drink-and-be-merry follow a materialistic view of life. Their activities are guided by it. There is a system of beliefs in every person's life. Thus, one's perception of life's purpose, ways to achieve such goal, relationship between various components of life, etc. become source-spring of all actions. The life styles and activities of people are good indicators of philosophy of life, eventhough people holding them may not consciously recognise so. So, everyone needs sets of values, perception of self and the world to make sense of life's purpose. Such perceptions can become motive for committed action. Thus, there is some link between philosophy and practice. There is, of course, need to consciously recognise the value systems to resolve contradictory situations. Philosophy then can become a working tool for improving practice.

PHILOSOPHY OF EXTENSION

Extension Education has become an important intervention in most parts of the world to develop rural areas. It is one of the arms of the national governments. Of late, the World Bank has provided new impetus through generous funding and encouraged structural changes in extension organisation. No doubt, role of extension is increasingly being recognised. At the same time, index fingers are being raised about the manner in which extension work is being performed. It is in the midst of such allegations and tremendous changes in socio-economic fabric of developing nations, technology, social theories and political conditions that one is apt to question once again what is philosophy of extension. What is the ultimate purpose of extension? How can one achieve the goals of extension? What is role of extension professionals in the process?

Extension as it developed in the nineteenth century, in the United States of America, contained the concerns of philosophers and philanthropists of the time. Philosophy of extension must have been influenced by the values, knowledge and situations existing during those times. Butt (1961) has explained carefully in one of the most popular text-books in India (Extension Education in Community Development), that material things are important only if they are useful to people. It is not the increased production or quantity of grains but people who are to be fed that ultimately matters. It is not the worldly goods but betterment in all aspects of human beings that really matters. It is not individual alone but the community which is of concern. In nutshell, the changes to be brought about must be based on scientific methods to ameliorate the rural problems. At the same time vlues of human dignity, self-reliance, freedom and moral responsibility cannot be ignored. The basic philosophy of extension work is directed at the conversion of the whole man. Changes in all aspects of human life through education is the goal. This is the approach to secure whole hearted co-operation of a person. Education cannot be substituted by mere dissemination of knowledge but changes must influence attitudes and modes of thinking and doing as well.

Kelsey and Hearne (1963) have also highlighted that philosophy of extension work is based on importance of individual in the promotion of progress for rural people and for the nation. Extension educators work with the people to help them develop themselves to achieve superior personal well-being. Together, they establish specific objectives expressed in terms of everyday living in the direction of overall objectives. Progress varies with individual needs, interests and abilities. During the process the whole community improves as a result of co-operative participation and leadership development. Extension Education is not only teaching people individual practices but also the interdependence of activities. Extension Education aims at developing comprehensive plans including home, family and community and then seeing that plan is carried out into action. Extension's specific job is furnishing the inspiration, specific advice, technical help and counselling to see that the people as individual, groups and communities work together as unit in blueprinting their own problems, charting their own courses and launch forth to achieve their objectives.

THE ESSENCE OF EXTENSION

The philosophy of extension work as enunciated by Butt, Esminger, Kelsey and Hearne, etc. has common concern for overall development of individuals, family and community. Education has been regarded as democratic tool to make people conscious of their problems. Co-operation and participation of people in their own development is essential. Keeping in view local culture, resources needs and interests, common goals can be formulated. People can be motivated to work to organise themselves to achieve them. In order to bring about overall development, use of science and technology and development of leadership are helpful. It is not only technology but also human values of dignity, self-respect, freedom that counts. There is no limit to the subject-matter areas of extension education. The moral responsibility of the people must be emphasized so as to bring desirable changes. Thus, it can be said that extension work concerns itself with people and their development, materials are only means to this end. The goal of development is all-sided rather than one sided. It is not the development of an individual also but that of community which is emphasized. Use of science rather than tradition is encouraged. People's co-operation and participation in carrying out self-created plan is the basis of such development.

It is thus clear that extension is not merely supply and service agency, to decide for rural people about what is good. It is not a short-cut to achieve material progress. It is neither doing things for local people by outside agency nor make people agree somehow what they do not like or need. Imposition or forceful persuasion is not the way of extension work. Above all extension is not the tool of publicity and propaganda for the government or technological institution. Putting the two together, philosophy of extension resounds similar to the ideals of religious scriptures. It is quite in keeping with the greater values of human development.

Various Approaches of Extension Work

Extension work is conducted around the world in a variety of ways. Each approach has its own basic assumption, structure and set of activities, as discussed below :

Technology/Research Centred Extension

In most cases extension work is viewed as vehicle for distributing pre-decided research findings to the clientele. It has its emphasis on findings available at the research centre. The unique circumstances or constraints at the farmers' end are often ignored or not considered.

Commodity Focussed Approach

This approach is quite popular in Western Africa where set of activities are geared to accelerate production of a single crop. Technical, administrative and input requirements for such crops are managed by board or private company. Technical messages are systematically conveyed to the farmers. There is provision for inputs, marketing of outputs, prompt payment for output etc.

Community Development Approach

This was the approach launched in India in 1952. This approach covers all aspects of rural life viz. agriculture, family planning, health, education, illiteracy, etc. This broadens the responsibilities of extension workers. The wide-ranging set of duties results in low performance, lack of mobility and confused supervision. The knowledge and ability of farmers to contribute towards the generation or improvisation of technology is never appreciated.

Extension as merely Advisory Function

Under such approach, it is assumed that the role of extension worker is to advise clientele what to do or what not to do. Extension worker does not have any other involvement.

Service or Supply Approach

The extension organisation provides information on crops and livestock. Besides, it also arranges for supply of inputs such as fertilizers and seeds. Many Asian countries follow such approach. Extension workers are overburdened with supply function. Due to lack of well developed infrastructure such provisions work as incentive.

Training and Visit System
This is an organised effort overcoming the lacunae of weak management. The approach mobilises the entire extension apparatus and research system for systematic and effective extension work. It promotes regularity of training, systematic visits by extension workers, effective supervision and technical recommendations. There is enhanced research-extension linkages.

Classical Extension Education Approach
The classical extension education approach that evolved in U.S.A. and was taken to different countries assumed that extension service can transform static rural economy in a dynamic one. It used variety of extension methods to convey for communication of information. Involvement of local leaders and participation of whole family was encouraged in this approach. There was considerable emphasis on training of women and youth as well.

Critiques on Extension Approach and Methods
No matter how ideal philosophy of extension may sound, the manner of implementing extension programmes have met with severe criticisms. Over a century or more since inception, extension work has taken many forms from purely community development to transfer of technology programmes. Many serious allegations have been made, of late about nature of extension organisation, focus on technology methods of communication, etc. as given below.

Extension Bureaucracy
Extension organisations are mostly parts of government departments. Thus, they follow similar organisational hierarchy, working condition and procedures as in the government. The plans and programmes are decided at the top rung of hierarchy and implemented at the grassroots. The need, interest and willingness of farmers are relegated to the background in a bid to fulfil pre-decided target.

Techno-centric Work
The thrust of most extension organisations these days seem to be the dissemination of technologies. Most of the technologies benefit the rsource-rich farmers and areas/regions with favourable infrastructure. Should extension become advocates of technologies without considering their consequences? Should the users of technology be considered first

4. *Sharing results*
Communication of results with other local and scientific networks to scrutinize and interpret them and incite others to adopt and test.

5. *Sustaining and consolidating system of PTD*
Creating favourable conditions for farmers' organisations, local institutions and support at policy level. Establishing physical infrastructure and other facilities for local experiment and management of research.

These steps are only suggestive and not rigid. PTD is still evolving organisational development, training and other institutional issues.

Rapid Rural Appraisal (RRA)

Rationale
Planning for rural development requires authentic information to provide right solution. Experiences of development in past showed that experts need better method to collect accurate and relevant information. Short visits to rural areas or lengthy surveys often do not provide the realistic picture of the situation. In order to meet such needs, RRA evolved as cost-effective and appropriate approach. Thus, RRAs came to be handy tool for collecting local insight and quality information needed for experts from outside to plan solutions to rural problems. These methods valued traditional knowledge and wisdom of people which local people possess naturally as they belong to the culture outsiders can easily obtain these through RRA.

What is RRA?
RRA is a way of collecting and analyzing information from field in short period of time. RRA uses multiple methods and involves people to collect and validate information and does not rest on anyone method.

Special features

1. Use of RRA demands respect for ITK.
Local people operate in the existing situation by virtue of their understanding of the environment. They have their own reasons and approach to cope with the situation. Experts must feel respect for basic knowledge that people possess.

human conduct, with respect to rightness or wrongness of certain actions and to the goodness or badness of the motives and ends of such action (Random House Dictionary of English Language, 1973). In deciding the canons of rightness it is not the goal or motive alone which matters but also the means through which goals are attained. Social ethics of development aims at good of the greatest number of people. However, should it exclude the happiness of individuals. What is good for group may not be good for individuals? Who can define the greater happiness of one and all, the change agent or the individual himself. Should change agent take initiative to decide on behalf of the ignorant majority?

Values and beliefs are not static entities. Dominant social thoughts and situation affect values. It is a common knowledge that application of sicence and evolutions of new technologies were triggered in the nineteenth century in order to meet the needs of the society. The resulting material prosperity and control over nature brought respectability for science and technology. The concern for material development, market economy, centralized, bureaucratic organisations and confidence in science were the order of the past century. With massive changes in technologies, their consequent effect on nature and social life have forced people to search for alternate means to development. There is clarion call for popular participation of people at all levels, non-hierarchal organisations with work-team, concern for nature, limited natural resources, equity and quality of life. Alternative concepts on development have shifted the focus of development on individuals, local culture, resource and sustainability rather than mere quantitative macro economic development. Considering that rural clientele in majority of Third World nation have limited education, access to resources, information about resources, motivation to develop, power to influence various forces of development and insights into problems, should extension take expert's position to dispense knowledge. Can it solve all the problems of the area? What should be the approach in the light of the emerging values?

Extension Education is basically an educational process drawing its insights from adult education. In this sense the importance of individuals, their right to choose a course of life must not be lost sight of. Role of extension should be one to help in personal growth and development of individuals. According to humanist philosophy, man is a conscious being capable of making choice and accordingly bring changes. Man is both cause and consequence of development. Individual alone has responsibility to decide and make efforts to fulfil possibilities. Thus, the educator has to resist tendencies to prescribe solutions. Participatory approach of education facilitating discussion, analysis and application of choices can lead to more fulfilling development. Problem solving experiential learning can help in developing initiatives of people. Even choice of technology should not be guided by the criteria of increasing production alone.

PRINCIPLES AND PROCEDURES OF EXTENSION WORK

How should extension work be carried out? The philosophical background and existing reality suggest that extension should be treated as planned educational activity for overall development of rural communities with the use of science and technology. No extension professional can afford to treat it as a random affair. The challenge of Human Resource Development in rural areas calls for inclusion of participatory approaches in planning, executing and evaluating extension works. It demands sensitivity and inter-disciplinary orientation on the part of extension educators to ward off untoward effects.

Extension work must be guided by time-tested principles of extension. Principles are guidelines for consistent action. They have evolved out of series of rigorous testing of theories in various settings. Principles of extension education have been applied and tested in many countries of the world for a long time. Some of them have more or less general application. Therefore, they are of use to extension workers. Principles of extension education have been elaborated below :

Principles of Need and Interest

The first principle of extension education outlines the basis for designing extension programme. Extension programmes should be based on needs and interest of the people. Need is gap between 'what is' and 'what ought to be' i.e. gap between the present situation and the possible situation. Thus, needs of the people are of prime concern for initiating an extension programme. Interest denotes atention with concern. People are at the centre of all extension works. Needs are of different types like physical needs (Food, clothing, housing etc.), social needs (affection, belonging) and integrative needs (Philosophy of life, spiritual need). Similarly needs may be classified as felt and unfelt. Felt needs are those which have been consciously identified by the individuals. We take felt needs as a starting point in extension work. No doubt there are other human needs as well viz. psychological, aesthetic and spiritual. Needs give reasons why people ought to pay heed. Alert extension worker should move in the direction of critical need to make programmes relevant. Interests indicate aspiration of people. Though not all needs and interests are developmental, extension workers must deal with the felt needs to begin with.

Principle of Cultural Difference

This principle underlines the importance of culture in extension work. Extension worker must have very high degree of sensitivity to acquaint himself with various aspects of beliefs, norms, values and views of people. The importance people give to things varies from place to place. Similarly, there are many do's and don'ts related with various aspects of living, working and doing. Extension worker as a change agent should immerse himself in the rural socio-cultural setting to be able to do culturally right things and devise programmes without offending values of people. This also relates to manner of working and behaving. Many societies pay lot of respect to elders, grains, or tools and greet them. Similar sensitivity should be reflected in content of programmes as well.

Extension programmes should be in consistence with the religious norms, beliefs, values and outlook of people of the area. Rural people are very rigid about their way of life and resist any departure from the set norms. It is thus essential that extension programmes should not offend the values of people. It is difficult to run a poultry programme in the Brahmin villages. Similarly, no good programme of piggery development can be successful amongst Muslim communities. There are many examples of insensitivity to local culture and wisdom in past. Thus a conscious extension worker should take time to live and learn before starting actual extension work.

Principle of Cultural Change

This principle lays importance on changing nature of the societies. Culture includes everything a man thinks, does or possesses. The culture is not static entity. It is ever changing due to a variety of forces. Outsiders do not realize that villages ever change because often there is little outward change as compared with urban areas. This is not true. All villages are not alike all the times. Villages do not remain static, they change. Thus all new learning must be built upon what has already been learnt. Extension worker must know the present level of knowledge and skills about any technology among farmers. What is good and important for one area may not be good and useful elsewhere. Thus the particular technological and other changes of each area must be known before formulating an extension programme.

Principles of Grassroot Organisation

Extension work cannot be done in vacuum. It requires basic organisation at the village level so that needs and aspirations of the people may be known, articulated and built into the programme. This will give strong foundation to all development programmes. Planning from below is key to all successful programmes. People and their problems should be represented appropriately. Then the involvement of community in decision making and collective action can be ensured. Planning for development calls for creating community structures to help people with homogeneous needs and problems to unite together and plan action. Extension worker can play catalytic role by mobilising the group and teaching them methods of working together.

Principles of Co-operation and Participation

Participation of people is fundamental requirement for any development work. It is people for whom the work has to be done. Thus, they must be motivated to come forward and co-operate at all stages of development work. If people co-operate and get involved, extension work is effective.

Principles of Leadership

Leader is one who exerts influence over other members of the group. Local leaders command respect and the average farmers seek their advice. In traditional rural societies nothing moves without head man's permission. Leaders are of different types. While working for promotion of change, leaders must be taken into confidence to influence others. Leaders, in some cases, may be further trained through meetings, field trips, group activities, etc. Voluntary leaders should be trained to take initiative in development of villages and multiply extension efforts. Voluntary leaders should be secular, scientific and community oriented.

Principle of Learning by doing

One learns better by actually being involved in the task. This gives practical experience and grip on the new skills to be learnt. The learner gains confidence which cannot be acquired by reading shelves of books. All practical skills are best learnt by performing. Thus, extension work must provide opportunities of actual involvement and help in reflecting over the experience.

Principle of Adaptability of Extension Methods

Extension workers have a range of options to choose from as far as extension methods and communication media are concerned. All the methods do not fit with all teaching situations. The context and purpose for which they are to be used form the basis for choice of methods. The constitution of the target groups, their education, past exposure to methods and media, preferences, etc. affect the process of selection. Villages may not have electricity. Thus, despite the audio-visual appeal, television may not work in the villages. Literacy is another barrier. Cultural contexts also guide the form or mode of presentation. Often, references are made about an extension worker who was teaching African audiences how to prevent Malaria through enlarged visual of mosquito. The audience did not think they had any reason to fear as such large mosquito are never seen in the locality. Many popular techniques of films or television will become meaningless to audiences who are not exposed to them. Besides, the mass-media do not always carry credibility.

Principle of Whole Family Inclusion

Extension work concerns the entire farming family consisting of farmers, farm women and farm youths. The entire family is involved in decision making as well as use of the farm products. Hence, it would be incomplete to formulate extension programme from the point of view of farmers alone. The housewives and children also carry out part of farming operation. Thus, their needs and aspiration also count significantly. Many a sound looking technology did not find application at the farms beyond trial stage because housewives were not taken into confidence. Now that it has been established beyond doubt that rural women share most of the tasks in farming, their involvement in extension programme has been duly considered in World Bank supported TV system.

Principle of Evaluation

Evaluation means assessment of merits and demerits of programme, person or thing. Evaluation refers to assessment of strengths and weaknesses of a programme, person or thing. It is a process of determining the value. It is a process of determining success or failure of a programme. Evaluation is one of the essential parts of extension work. There must be provision to evaluate an extension programme periodically in order to bring about improvement in the programme and recast the programme in the light of evaluation results.

Extension work aims to bring changes in human behaviour. Evaluation can be carried out periodically at different points of time. Evaluation before designing the programme or baseline survey helps in finding content and methods for programme. Evaluation during the process of programme implementation is known as monitoring. Monitoring helps in keeping track of the progress in relation to what was planned. Monitoring helps in providing precise information. It can standardise the content and programme. Standard methods of collecting accurate information on field activities need to be used. Evaluation at the end of a programme gives ideas about the gains from extension programme. However, impact of the programmes can be determined after lapse of some time the long term impact.

Evaluation can be done through a range of methods like observation, survey, group discussion, tests, etc. Precise information can be gathered by administering standard tests. Use of sampling design and controlled experiments give availability to the data gathered. Case studies can provide descriptive information.

Principle of Satisfaction

The ultimate objective of all extension programme is satisfaction of people with whom work is done. If the result of adoption of new technology is not satisfying, farmers will lose faith in it. Extension worker will also lose credibility. On the other hand if the reward is satisfying, farmers will follow and adopt new technology.

PROCEDURE OF EXTENSION WORK

Extension education aims to bring qualitative improvement in rural living. Thus, irrespective of the form or goal of organisation, it should endeavour to develop precious human resource by creating appropriate environment, providing motivation and technical support for self-reliant growth. In this process extension practitioner ceases to be an expert or traditional teacher. He is more of a facilitator or catalyst to help the members of community in understanding problems, organising self-help group, training of leaders, linkage with outside agencies and management of development activities. How can extension help in realisation of existing problems. After all, it is people who have to rise and do something to ameliorate their lot. Extension can serve as a catalyst. It can initiate a process of dialogue with the people. Such dialogic communication are possible only in an atmosphere of trust, empathy and openness.

People have their own systems of beliefs, values and traditional channels of communication. Extension practitioner can identify such natural forum to initiate process of exploration about existing local problems. Techniques of encouraging discussion on needs and problems depend on the cultural context. It takes time for the practitioner to live and acquaint himself with the cultural content. It is not a matter of knowing language alone but also perception of people, socio-cultural environment, political factors, economic situation, opportunities and constraints. In fact, the practitioner should first immerse himself in the community before undertaking his role as catalyst. In order to work effectively extension workers must undertake the following activities.

Problem Analysis

Extension worker is more of a facilitator. He is a helpful, sensitive and humble human guide to help people visualise their situation more critically than before. People have wisdom to cope with problems. They must be provoked to reflect on the existing realities in more analytical manner through probing questions on socio-economic situation. It is essential to enhance awareness of problems to inspire action. Extension worker, thus, tries to awaken people and train them to decide appropriate action programme. Many development projects have used the approach popularly known as conscientisation. In Bangladesh, Proshika Manobik Unnayan Kendra Project developed rural poor to take part in participatory action research to visualise their problems and devise solutions. Later, they were helped to gain productive skills and organise economic enterprises.

Local Organisations

People's participation is possible only when organisational structures are devised to take care of problems of different groups within a community. It is better to consider all the people, all the issues and total geographical area of the community through appropriate representative groups. Villages may have some traditional organisation structure such as village club or Gram Sabha. At some places self-help groups may have to be organised. Vaishali Area Small Farmers Association (VASFA) project in Vaishali, Bihar has shown how small and marginal farmers can be organised into self-managed groups to pull their fragmented land together to develop common productive assets. The group increased their cultivation several times by availing credit, irrigation, inputs and technical advice through the registered societies of homogeneous members. Regular meetings, demonstration, training, etc. were means to decide collective actions.

Thus, people can participate in building plans for the future of some kind of village structure is created to co-ordinate and implement the plans.

Local Level Planning

People have knowledge about their own communities. They are in better position to resolve local problems. They should be helped with methods to work together. Village plans prepared by people, who know their resources, infrastructure and development mechanism, have a sense of realism. Besides, people have a sense of responsibility in executing them. Such plans are more sustainable than those made by outsiders. Such responsibility in decision making can enhance leadership. Grassroots planning utilises people's commonsense, their creative potentials and local resources most effectively. Besides, such plans address to the priority areas of emphasis, as perceived by the people.

Involvement of all sections of people ensures effective implementation as well. Institute of Cultural Affairs, India used village consultations in their rural development projects across Maharashtra. The consultation were a festive affair in the village and five days planning events were organised through discussion and team visits to village sites. People decided on future vision and make proposals to actualize them through tactical plans.

Leadership Development

In order to implement participatory methods of working with people, local leadership should be developed. In every community some people do have tendency to work for other. They influence peers due to personal abilities. Such people can be trained through practical work or engagement in community works. Methods of organising community structures leading meetings, building consensus and conducting planning sessions work. Seva Mandir in Udaipur, Rajasthan trained local volunteers in leadership skills to work as change agents for village development. Another voluntary organisation AWARE, orients village organisers in a 30-day programme by exposing them to ideology and methods of working in villages. Practical instructions are given on organising local association, conducting meetings, starting revolving funds, making use of government schemes, relevant laws, legal procedures, etc. They live in villages under supervisor and prepare detailed reports on the situation.

Self-management of Programme

It is ideal to help local organisation in carrying out programmes decided by themselves. Extension practitioner may help in providing needed training, technical information and linkage with development organisations and experts. However, responsibility for getting works done should lie on the leaders and community members. Regular meetings of various group to review progress and reports to general body can inculcate a sense of accountability among all concerned. Continuous training of core group of committed leader can foster self-confidence and ensure continuance of the programmes.

In Rural Multiplier Programme in Brazil, role of extension agent shifted from one of passing information to less educated peasants into one of active dialogue with the farmers over the possible application of techniques facilitated by village multiplier. Multiplier, who is a member from the village community, is selected due to his leadership characteristics. He works with the community to discuss the problems and generation of alternative solutions. The solution are then implemented by the community.

REFERENCES

Butt, H. W. (1961). Principles and Philosophy of Extension Education. In *Extension Education in Community Development,* New Delhi, Directorate of Extension, Ministry of Food & Agriculture, Government of India.

Esminger (1957). *Guide to Community Development and Cooperation,* Government of India, New Delhi.

ICA (1984). Learning and Education Process, the IERD Co-ordination Centre, Rue Amedee Lymen Stroat, 8, 1030. Brussels, Belgium.

Kelsey, L.D. & Hearne, C.C. (1967). *Cooperative Extension Work,* Cornell University Press, Ithaca, New York.

BIBLIOGRAPHY

Adhikarya. R. and R. D. Colle (1983). Reaching out : The Role of Audio Cassette Communication in Rural Development, Occasional paper No. 19, Asian Mass Communication Research and Information Centre, Singapore.

Appa Rao. G (1991). Interactive Video — An Innovative Training Method, *Agricultural Extension Review,* 3(5).

Ban, A. W. Vanden (1982). The Challenges of Agricultural Extension In 1980's. *Indian Journal of Extension Education,* 17 (3 & 4), pp. 1-9.

Bhasin, K. (1985). There is no music in Agricultural Extension, *Ceres,* 18 (4).

Brown, M. (1965). Professional values. *Journal of Co-operative Extension Service* 3(2), pp. 67-74.

Butt, H. W. (1961). Principles and Philosophy of Extension Education in *Extension Education in Community Development,* New Delhi, Directorate of Extension, Ministry of Food and Agriculture, Government of India.

Carrol, J. (1982). Teleconferencing, *Dun's Business Month,* C I X No. 1/ 1982, pp. 130-134.

Chambers. R. (1980). Small farmer is a professional, *Ceres,* 13 (1) 1980, pp. 19-23.

Chambers, R. (1990). Microenvironments unobserved Gate Keeper Series No. 22, published by the Sustainable Agriculture Programme of the International Institute for Environment and Development, London, U. K.

Chambers, R. (1991). To make the flip strategies for working with undervalued resource agriculture, Participatory Technology Development in Sustainable Agriculture, In *ILIEA,* 1991.

Clark, R.C. (1965). Extension Education as profession , *Indian Journal of Extension Education.* 1(1) pp. 9-13.

Colin, R. (1971) Education from within, *Ceres,* 4 (3), pp. 41-45.

Colle, Royal. (1975). ACT : A New Kind of Communication. *Educational Broadcasting International,* The British Council. Vol . 8.

Dahama, O. P. and Bhatnagar, O. P. (1987). *Education and Communication for Development,* Oxford & IBH Publishing Co, New Delhi.

Dahama, O.P. *Extension and Rural Welfare*, Ram Krishna & Sons, Agra.

Dasgupta, D.D. (1993). Traditional wisdom and experience in Agro-technology generation and use, paper presented in XVII Indian Social Science. Congress, August 10-15, 1993, Bangalore.

Esminger, D. (1957). *Guide to Community Development and Co-operation*, Government of India, New Delhi.

Fort, W. (1984). A Primer on interactive video *A. V. Video*, pp. 29-41.

Freiri, P. (1971). Knowledge is critical appraisal of the world, *Ceres*, 4 (3), pp. 46-51.

Gupta, A. K. (1990). Documenting Indigenous Farmers' Practices, *ILIEA Newsletter*, 6(2), pp. 29-30.

Gupta; S. L.; Singh, S. P.; and Dubey, V. K. (1994). Traditional wisdom : A conceptual exploration, *Interaction*, 12(1), 1994.

Gupta, V. S. (1984). Farm Journalism—the Indian Perspective, paper presented at the National Seminar on Agricultural Journalism : Problems & Prospects held on March 27-29, 1984 at G.B.P.U.A. & T., Pantnagar.

Haiman, F. S. (1950). *Group Leadership and Democratic Action*. Houghton Mifflin Company, New York.

Havercort, B.; Hiemstra, W.; Reijntjes, C. and Essers, S. (1991). Strengthening Farmers' capacity for technology development, *ILIEA*, 4 (3), 1991.

Havlock, Ronald. G. (1973). Planning for Innovation through Dissemination and Utilization of Knowledge, Centre for Research on Utilization of Scientific Knowledge, Univ. of Mich. Ann. Arbor, Mich. Univ. of Michigan.

Hynka, O. (1979). Four Single Page Learning Model, *A. V. Instruction*, April 1979.

I.L.O. (1986). Vocational Training, Glossary of Selected Terms of International Labour Office, Geneva.

Iffner, P. L. and A. F. Douds (1988). *Train-the Trainer — Practical Skills that work*, HRD Press, Massachusetts, U.S.A.

Jhamtani, A. and Singh, Y. P. (1980). Directory of Degree Research in Extension (1972-78). *Division of Agricultural Extension*, Indian Agricultural Research Institute, New-Delhi-110012.

Kelsey, L. D. and Hearne, C. C. (1967). *Co-operative Extension Work*, Cornell University Press, Ithaca, New York.

Kumar, B. and Roy, N. K. Towards more participative and developmental broadcasting, *Interaction*, 6 (1 & 2).

Kumar, B. and Singh, K. Developmental use of video—some experiences in the book, *Video for Rural Development*, (Eds.) Hansra, B.S. and Mathur, P. N., 1991. Classical Pub. Co., New Delhi.

Kumar, B. and Singh, K. Journal for Farmers, *Vidura,* Sep-Oct, 25 (5), 1988, pp. 15.

Kumar, B. and Singh, K. Video technology and changing development scenario a third world perspective, *Interaction* 6(1 & 2) 1988.

Leagans, J. Paul (1971). Extension Education and Modernisation in Leagans and Loomis (Eds.) *Behavioural Change in Agriculture, Concepts and Strategies for Influencing Transition.*

Lowdermilk, M. K. (1985). A System Process for Improving the quality of Agricultural Extension, *Journal of Extension Systems.* 1 : 45-53, December.

Lynton, R. P. and Pareek, U. (1967). *Training for Development,* Illinois, Richard, D. Irwin Inc.

Lynton, R. P. and Pareek, U. (1990). *Training for Development,* Sage Publications, New Delhi.

Malhan, P. N. (1977). Where is Rural Press, *Vidura,* 14 (2), 1977.

Mata, N. (1992). CTTA; A. Method for transferring technology to farmers. *Planning and Implementation Guide,* Academy for Educational Development, USA.

McDermott. The Technology of Technological Innovations, A Model of Technology Development Testing Adaptation and Integral Function, *Journal of Extension System,* 4(1) 88, p. 7-28.

Mehta, P. (1983). New extension and training strategies, *Indian Journal of Extension Education,* 19 (1 & 2), 1983, pp. 1-14.

Mishra, D. C. (1990). *New Directions in Extension Training,* Directorate of Extension, Department of Agriculture and Co-operation, Ministry of Agriculture, New Delhi.

Mishra, D. C. Defining Agricultural Extension for 1990's, Directorate of Extension occasional paper I, Directorate of Extension, Department of Agriculture and Co-operation, Ministry of Agriculture, New Delhi.

Modi, B. Energizing the communication component in extension—A case for new pilot project, paper presented at the World Bank symposium, 1992.

Mosher, A. (1978). An Introduction to Agricultural Extension, New York, Agricultural Development Council (ADC), Singapore University Press.

Mundy, P. and Crompton, L. (1991). Indigenous Communication and Indigenous Knowledge, *Development Communication Report,* 74 (3), pp. 1-3.

Nadler, L. (1994). Human Resource Development in Leonard Nadler (ed.) : The *Handbook of Human Resource Development,* John Wiley & Sons, New York, pp. 1.16 to 1.22.

Nieuwsma, Lyonette (1984). AGNET-increasing its effectiveness, *Journal of*

Extension Systems, May-June, Vol. 22, pp. 11-15.

Radhakrishna, R. B.; A.W. Elting & Brown, B. E. (1993). Training of Farmers and Extension Personnel in Samanta, R. K. (Ed.) *Extension Strategy for Agricultural Development in 21st Century*; Mittal Publications; New Delhi.

Raman, K. V. (1988). FSR — its implications in future research studies in India, *Farming Systems Research Newsletter*. 2 (2) 3-5.

Raman, K. V. and Balaguru, T. (1992). Farming systems research in India, *NAARM*, Hyderabad.

Rao, V.P. (1992) Human Resource Development and Training, *MDI Management Journal,* 15(1), pp. 108-111.

Reddy, A. A. (1974). *Extension Education Prasar*, 2 (3).

Reddy, S. V. and Sahay, B. N. (1971). Pattern of farm leaders identified in a progressive and non-progressive village, *Indian Journal of Extension Education,* 7 (3 & 4), pp. 117-123.

Reddy, S.V. and Sahay, B. N. (1973). Differential characteristics of farm leaders in a progressive and non-progressive village, *Indian Journal of Extension Education,* 9 (3 & 4), pp. 87-91.

Rhoades, R. E. and Boothe, R. H. (1982). Farmer-Back-to-Farmer : A Model for Generating Acceptable Agricultural Technology, Agricultural Administration.

Rogan, R. G., Gary A. Simmons, Teleconferencing. *Journal of Extension Systems,* Vol. 22. No. Sep-Oct 1984, pp. 27-33.

Rolling, N. (1974). From theory to action. *Ceres,* 7 (5) pp. 22-24.

Rolling, N. (1979). The Logic of Extension, *Indian Journal of Extension Education.*

Rolling, N. (1984). Appropriate opportunities and technology, *Ceres,* 17 (1) pp. 219.

Rolling, N. (1986). *Extension Science-Information System in Agricultural Development,* The Edinburg, Cambridge University Press.

Rolling, N. (1988). *Extension Science : Information Systems in Agricultural Development,* Cambridge University Press.

Saville, A. N. (1965). Extension in Rural communities : *A Manual for Agriculture and Home Extension Workers,* London, Oxford University Press, Reprinted 1986, Oxford Tropical Handbook.

Shukla, A. N. (1972). The Concept of Extension Education—A study in Psycho-Physical Methods in P.R.R. Sinha (Ed.). *Studies in Extension Education,* National Institute of Community Development, Hyderabad.

Singh, K. N. (1982). Challenges of Extension in Eighties, *Indian Journal of Extension Education,* 17 (1 & 2), pp. 1-9.

Singh, K. N. (1980). Agricultural Extension Education in ICAR, In *Handbook of Agriculture*, Chapter 16, p. 703.

Sinha, P. R. R. (Ed.) (1972). *Studies in Extension Education*, Hyderabad, National Institute of Community Development (NICD).

Sinha, P. R. R. (1973). Role of extension education in Farmers' Organisation in Agricultural Development — A critical analysis, *Community Development and Panchayati Raj*, 5 (1), pp. 8-19.

Strayton, R. (1986). Organisation of courses and conferences in *ILO*, chapter 27, International Labour Organisation, Geneva.

Supe, S. V. (1983). *An Introduction to Extension Education*, New Delhi, Oxford and IBH, second printing 1984.

Swanson, Burton, E. Ed. 1984 . *Agricultural Extension — A Reference Manual*, Rome, Food and Agricultural Organization (FAO) of the United Nations, Second edition.

Tuazon, R.R. (1991) Bridging the gap in rural extension work. *Agricultural Information Development Bulletin*, 13(4), pp. 220.

Tead, O. (1951), *The Art of Administration*, McGraw Hill, New York.

Vaishampayan, J. V. (1996). Extension—the third dimension of higher education, *University News*, 34 (5) 1996, pp. 6-8.

Walker, M. (1994). Agricultural Information system, synergy and Development, *Journal of Extension System*, 10(20), Dec. 1994.

White, B.A. and Brockett, R. G. Putting Philosophy into Practice, *Journal of Extension*, Vol. 25, 1987.

INDEX